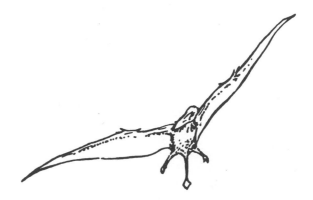

Dinosaurs

John C. Kricher

Illustrated by Gordon Morrison

Sponsored by the
National Wildlife Federation
and the Roger Tory Peterson Institute

HOUGHTON MIFFLIN HARCOURT   BOSTON • NEW YORK

W9-AGB-601

To Dustin Hanna, J. Seth Morrison,
and Scott Scheffey — three guys who
like dinosaurs.

For permission to reproduce selections
from this book, write to Permissions,
Houghton Mifflin Harcourt Company,
215 Park Avenue South, New York,
New York 10003.

Visit our website:
www.hmhbooks.com

ISBN 987-0-544-03255-2

Printed in China

SCP 10 9 8 7 6 5 4 3 2 1

INTRODUCTION

The world of the dinosaurs is one we can only imagine. These magnificent creatures have been extinct for many millions of years. Today we marvel in watching reptiles and birds, living legacies of the dinosaurs, and in visiting the great natural history museums that house the remains of the once abundant dinosaurs. We wonder: What did dinosaurs look like when skin and muscle covered their giant bones? How did they behave? Were they colorful? With interest in dinosaurs perhaps higher today than at any other time since their discovery, this coloring book should serve well to introduce you to these amazing creatures.

Because no person (except in the imaginations of Hollywood movie directors) has ever seen a living *Tyrannosaurus,* or any other kind of dinosaur, we can only guess as to how they were colored. However, by looking at mammals, birds, and reptiles, and with an educated imagination, we can, in our mind's eye, breathe life into these long-gone denizens of ancient forests and swamps. By visiting museums to see firsthand the remains of dinosaurs and then using this coloring book, you will sharpen your observations as you learn to think of these magnificent animals as they once were, living and dynamic.

The text by John C. Kricher includes the latest information available on dinosaur anatomy, behavior, and ecology. The scenes of life during the dinosaur era depict, as accurately as possible, both the plant life and animal life of the time. The dinosaurs themselves, so artfully drawn by Gordon Morrison, are seen as energetic animals active in ways similar to modern birds and mammals. As in any field guide, the illustrations offer shortcuts to recognition. You'll soon know the plant eaters from the meat eaters and the sauropods from the stegosaurs.

Dinosaurs give us an exciting glimpse into the past history of our planet. Their size and diversity fascinate us. The extinction of the dinosaurs, still an event shrouded in mystery, can help teach us to value more the extraordinary animals and plants with which we share today's earth.

Most of you will find colored pencils best suited for coloring this book, but if you are handy with brushes and paints, you may prefer to fill in the outlines with watercolors. Crayons, too, can be used. But don't labor; have fun. Bring the dinosaurs and their kindred back to life.

Roger Tory Peterson

ABOUT THIS BOOK

Dinosaur watching. No person has ever seen a living dinosaur. It may seem odd to design a Field Guide Coloring Book for a group of creatures that have been extinct for 65 million years. A coloring book may seem especially odd since pigments do not leave any traces in the fossil record, and so we have no direct knowledge of dinosaurs' actual colors. However, it is challenging to try to reconstruct how dinosaurs may have looked, what color patterns they may have displayed, and how they lived. This challenge has been taken up by numerous scientists as well as by the general public. Dinosaurs are more in the public mind today than at any other time since their discovery in the early nineteenth century, just over 150 years ago. The world's great natural history museums, where dinosaur remains are on display, are attracting millions of visitors curious about the immense reptiles. Automated dinosaur models, some full-scale, delight crowds who gather to watch *Apatosaurus* raise its neck and turn its head, *Tyrannosaurus* open its cavernous mouth, and *Stegosaurus* swish its spike-laden tail.

It is a romantic notion to hope that somewhere on the planet, in some as-yet-unexplored forest or swamp, living dinosaurs still survive. Sir Arthur Conan Doyle's popular science fiction novel *The Lost World* was based on just this notion, as was the Hollywood film *Baby* (1985), which depicted the discovery and subsequent rescue of a juvenile brontosaur (see p. 20). Alas, however, the evidence indicates that dinosaurs are no more. It has been 65 million years since dinosaurs died out. They and their contemporaries were the ancestors of the animals found on the earth today. The world of the dinosaurs is, indeed, a lost world, but we do have their remains to inspire us as we contemplate them. We can study their skeletons and their fossilized tracks and infer how they moved. Some could run fast and even gallop, like modern mammals. Some could rear up on their hind legs. Some held their tails stiffly; others had whiplike tails, perhaps used to knock a would-be predator off balance. From study of their skulls and teeth, we learn that most ate plants but some devoured flesh. The width of their rib cages tells us about the positions of their internal organs and even gives us an idea of the size of their hearts. The position of their nostrils and the structure of their nasal passages help tell us about the sounds they may have made. By comparing dinosaur skeletons, footprints, and other fossils with modern reptiles, birds, and mammals, we can make educated guesses about dinosaur anatomy, movement, metabolism, digestion, reproduction, hunting behavior, and social lives. We can also make educated guesses about their colors.

For today's dinosaur watcher, the "field" is the museum and the library, as well as the outdoors. By observing dinosaur reconstructions in such museums as the American Museum of Natural History in New York, the Smithsonian Institution in Washington, D.C., the Field Museum of Natural History in Chicago, or the Royal Ontario Museum in Toronto, you can appreciate firsthand the diversity and size of these unique creatures. By visiting such sites as Dinosaur Provincial Park in Alberta, Canada, or Dinosaur National Monument in Utah, you can see dinosaur fossils still embedded in rock in places where they lived so many millions of years ago. And by studying the ecology of today's reptiles, birds, and mammals, you can make inferences about dinosaur ecology. With an educated mind and a creative outlook, a curiosity and enthusiasm for dinosaurs can become real knowledge about them. One of the best ways to take up the challenge to know the dinosaurs is to color them.

How to Use This Book

Coloring the drawings. In a way, coloring dinosaurs is an easy task. Since no one knows for certain what colors they were, nobody can say you're wrong no matter how you color them! However, before you get carried away, keep in mind that we do have some potential models on which to base our guesses about color. We can look at modern reptiles, for instance. Crocodiles and their relatives trace their ancestry back to when dinosaurs still ruled the planet. Perhaps some dinosaurs were colored greenish, or grayish brown, like modern crocodilians. Some dinosaurs may have had diamond patterning like that of many snakes, such as the pythons. We can also look at modern mammals as possible models. The largest dinosaurs were similar anatomically to elephants and rhinos. Perhaps they were darkly pigmented, like their mammalian counterparts. Some dinosaurs may have been strongly countershaded (light below, dark above) or have had stripes or other patterning that helped camouflage them in a forest. Some dinosaurs may have had colorful head patterning or body striping—adaptations perhaps for intimidating rivals or attracting mates.

In this book we have tried to use our imaginations in concert with present knowledge about dinosaur ecology to make suggestions as to how to color the drawings. The colors shown on the stickers are meant only as guides — *suggested* colors. You may copy our suggestions or create your own color patterns. We will likely never know if we've colored these dinosaurs correctly, but it's fun to try. However "correct" your colors, you will learn about the dinosaurs' shapes and structures as you color them in.

Introduction to the Dinosaurs

When dinosaurs lived. Dinosaurs were present on earth for approximately 150 million years, during a time named the Mesozoic era, or "Age of Middle Life" (see pp. 10–11). The Mesozoic era is divided into three periods, the Triassic, Jurassic, and Cretaceous. The Triassic period began about 225 million years ago, and dinosaurs evolved sometime during the early Triassic. The Jurassic period began 193 million years ago and lasted until the Cretaceous period, which began 136 million years ago. It was during the Jurassic and Cretaceous periods that dinosaurs prospered, comprising the dominant groups of terrestrial animals. All dinosaurs became extinct at the close of the Cretaceous period (or very shortly thereafter), 65 million years ago.

It is tempting to view dinosaurs as "failures" because all have become extinct. Such an opinion is mistaken. Primates, the mammal group to which humans belong, have been on the planet for barely 60 million years, less than half the tenure of dinosaurs. The apes have been in existence for only 35 million years, only about one-fourth the time span of the dinosaurs. Our most immediate ancestors, the australopithecines (see p. 63), are only about 3.5 million years old. Finally, our species, *Homo sapiens,* is a mere 500,000 years old — thus dinosaurs occupied prominent roles on earth for 300 times longer than we have to date! Such a duration hardly represents failure.

Dinosaurs may even still exist, in a manner of speaking. Studies of the earliest fossil bird, *Archaeopteryx* (see p. 40), link this species very closely with a group of small carnivorous (meat-eating) dinosaurs. Many scientists now believe that birds evolved *directly* from dinosaurs, and thus today's birds are really feathered dinosaurs. If this view is correct, our national bird, the bald eagle, is also our national dinosaur.

Dinosaur classification. Dinosaurs were reptiles, though they were very different from reptiles living today. There were two major groups of dinosaurs. One group, the saurischians, had hipbones arranged similarly to those of modern lizards; hence the name *lizard-hipped dinosaurs.* This group contained both plant eaters and meat eaters. The huge sauropods (see pp. 20–22 and 29), with their long necks and tiny heads, were all herbivores, or plant eaters, but the bipedal theropods (see pp. 23, 27, 38, and 52), which included the immense carnosaurs such as *Tyrannosaurus rex,* the slender ostrich dinosaurs (see p. 41), and the small but ferocious coelurosaurs (see pp. 19 and 42), were all carnivores (meat eaters). The other major dinosaur group, the ornithischians, had hipbones arranged somewhat like those of modern birds; hence the name *bird-hipped dinosaurs.* All of the bird-hipped dinosaurs were herbivores. Included in this

lizard-hipped
dinosaur

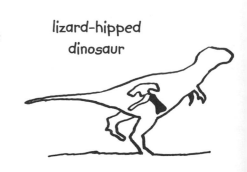

bird-hipped
dinosaur

group are the stegosaurs (see p. 26), the ornithopods (pp. 46 and 49–51), the ankylosaurs (p. 43), and the ceratopsians (pp. 47–48 and 53).

How dinosaurs may have lived. The earliest reconstructions of dinosaurs showed them as active animals similar to modern mammals. However, that view soon was replaced by one based more on comparisons of dinosaurs with today's reptiles — the turtles, snakes, lizards, and crocodiles. Dinosaurs were pictured as lumbering brutes, some of which were so large that they had to remain in water just to support their grotesquely large bodies. Because reptiles are cold-blooded, they cannot maintain a high internal body temperature, and are often sluggish, especially in cool temperatures. The sizes of dinosaurs, combined with the presumption that they functioned internally like lizards and crocodiles, gave rise to the belief that they lived "slow-motion" lives.

In more recent years dinosaurs have been viewed in a new light. Studies of dinosaur anatomy, such as the microscopic structure of dinosaur bone, reveal striking similarities to modern mammals. New methods of analyzing both their anatomy and community relationships suggest that some or even most dinosaurs may have been warm-blooded, like birds and mammals — capable of maintaining the high rate of metabolism typical of active animals.

The notion of "warm-blooded dinosaurs" has stimulated much study. The new view is that dinosaurs lived their lives much more like birds and mammals than like snakes and crocodiles. Dinosaurs may have hunted in packs, chasing down prey. They may have had elaborate courtship behaviors, like today's birds. Some nested in colonies, tending their young well after hatching. No longer considered lumbering giants, dinosaurs are now seen as sleeker, faster, and far more maneuverable than was previously believed. Though most dinosaurs probably had scaly or crocodile-like skin (some fossilized dinosaur skin has been found), some, especially the smaller ones, may have been covered by feathers — an aid in staying warm. The link between dinosaurs and birds (all of which are warm-blooded) is very strong.

The evidence is quite compelling that dinosaurs were active, often social animals. They show great diversity in body shape and in ways of moving, feeding, mating, and raising their young. They lived in a broad range of habitats throughout the world. The drawings by Gordon Morrison show dinosaurs as vital, dynamic creatures. Now you can use colors to bring them to life even more.

John C. Kricher

FOSSILS

Fossils *are the preserved remains or traces of life in the past. Embedded in rocks are the fossilized bones, teeth, shells, and other parts of ancient creatures. In most cases these parts have become stone, with minerals having gradually replaced what was once living tissue.*

Fossils are contained in rocks called **sedimentary rocks,** *which are formed of hardened sediments such as mud and sand. When plants and animals die and become buried in the sediments, they are sometimes preserved within the rock as fossils. As sediments are deposited over time, sedimentary rocks form in layers, the oldest on the bottom, the youngest on the top. Scientists can study the layers and see a record of life in ages long past.*

Trilobite To 2 feet. Trilobites, named for their three body lobes, thrived in the ancient oceans, becoming extinct before dinosaurs evolved. They were arthropods, related distantly to horseshoe crabs (see p. 12). Most were only a few inches long. They probably fed on small worms and other animals in the mud. (1)

Crinoid To 2 feet. Resembling flowers, crinoids are sometimes called "sea lilies." They are actually animals called echinoderms (spiny skin), related to sea stars and sea urchins. The flowerlike tentacles were used to capture tiny animals for food. Some crinoids exist today in the deep oceans. (2)

Solitary Coral To 6 inches. Today, corals make vast colonial reefs that support lush oceanic life in tropical waters. Many ancient corals were solitary, consisting of a single polyp surrounded

Trilobite

Crinoid

Solitary Coral

by tentacles to capture food. Only the hard outer covering of the polyp remains as a fossil. (3)

Brachiopod To 2 inches. Brachiopods look like clams. They were very abundant prior to the appearance of dinosaurs. A few still exist today (see p. 12), but most are extinct. They fed by opening their shells and capturing tiny prey with an elaborate tentacle. (4)

Ammonite To 3 feet. Ammonites are distantly related to the squids and chambered nautilus (see p. 12). They abounded in the sea during the dinosaurs' reign, only to become extinct along with the dinosaurs. All that remains of the ammonites are fossils of their elaborately coiled, ornately patterned shells. (5)

Eurypterid To 8 feet. Called "sea scorpions," these arthropods were probably the first predators of early fishes. Most eurypterids were small, but some real giants existed. All were extinct before dinosaurs appeared. (6)

Calamites To 100 feet. This ancient plant was a close relative of the small horsetails that occur along lakeshores. It lived long before dinosaurs appeared. Its remains are part of coal deposits, which we call "fossil fuels." (7)

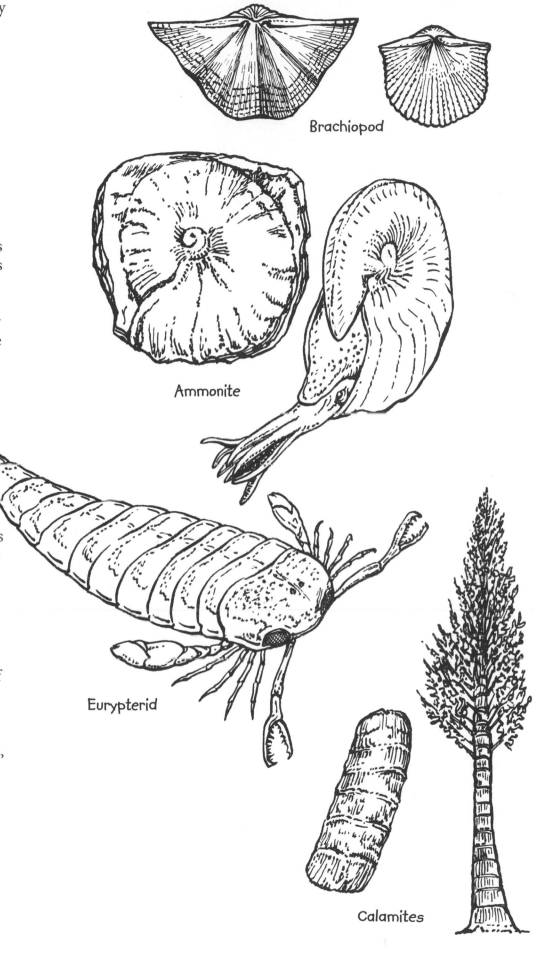

Brachiopod

Ammonite

Eurypterid

Calamites

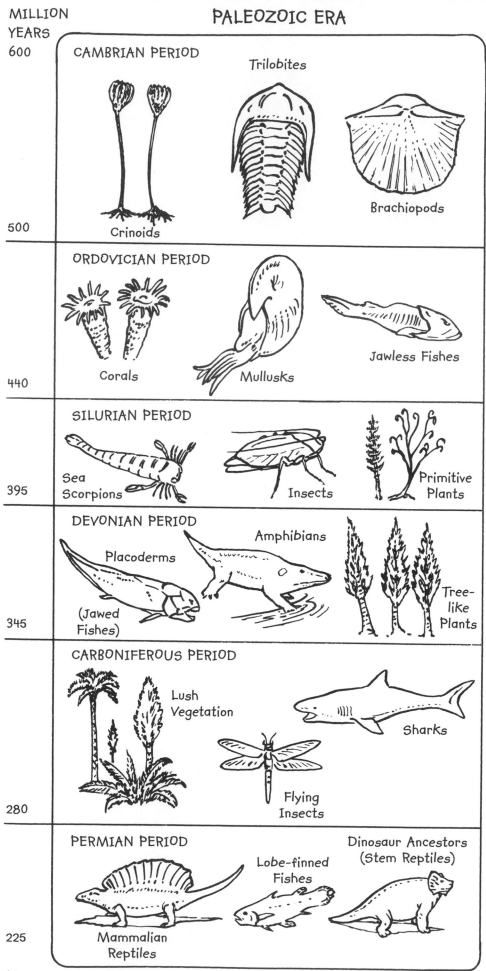

PALEOZOIC ERA

MILLION YEARS

600

CAMBRIAN PERIOD

Crinoids

Trilobites

Brachiopods

500

ORDOVICIAN PERIOD

Corals

Mullusks

Jawless Fishes

440

SILURIAN PERIOD

Sea Scorpions

Insects

Primitive Plants

395

DEVONIAN PERIOD

Placoderms (Jawed Fishes)

Amphibians

Tree-like Plants

345

CARBONIFEROUS PERIOD

Lush Vegetation

Flying Insects

Sharks

280

PERMIAN PERIOD

Mammalian Reptiles

Lobe-finned Fishes

Dinosaur Ancestors (Stem Reptiles)

225

GEOLOGIC TIME

Earth has a long history, which began when the planet formed about 4.6 billion years ago. Living organisms, quite similar in many respects to today's bacteria, were present nearly 3.5 billion years ago. However, complex life is much more "recent," having evolved in the sea less than a billion years ago. Later, some groups invaded land.

Scientists called paleontologists are geological historians. They study rocks that date back millions, sometimes billions, of years. These rocks contain fossils that are records of life in the past.

The figure of the paleontologist (the man in the hat) shown here appears next to some of the dinosaurs in this book, to give you a better idea of their relative size.

Geologists and paleontologists recognize that major changes have periodically occurred on earth, and thus they divide the history of earth into large chunks of time called eras. Eras are divided into smaller chunks called periods.

From 600 million years ago (when animals and plants first widely appeared) to the present there have been three geologic eras, named the Paleozoic (ancient life), Mesozoic (middle life), and Cenozoic (recent life). The Paleozoic era consisted of six periods, the Mesozoic of three periods, and the Cenozoic of two periods. We are still in the Cenozoic.

Paleontologist

PALEOZOIC ERA

This was a span of 375 million years before dinosaurs appeared. Life thrived in the seas, where corals, echinoderms (starfish and their relatives), segmented worms, clams, snails, squidlike mollusks, and many arthropods abounded. The trilobites and sea scorpions gazed upon the first backboned animals, fishes barely 3 inches in length. Sometime during the late Silurian period life invaded land. Primitive plants such as horsetails began to grow along ancient lake sides. Scorpions and cockroaches scurried across what was still a barren landscape. By the late Devonian period, air-breathing fish evolved into the first four-legged, backboned animals, the amphibians. Reptiles evolved from amphibians in the Carboniferous period, when great forests of lush vegetation covered the tropical earth. The end of the Permian period brought a massive extinction. Among the survivors were the ancestors of dinosaurs.

MESOZOIC ERA

The Mesozoic era was the Age of Reptiles. Giant dinosaurs stalked the earth, and huge aquatic reptiles swam the seas. Mammals evolved in the Triassic period, and birds evolved from dinosaurs in the Jurassic. The first flowering plants appeared. The Cretaceous probably ended with a dramatic cosmic event (see pp. 54–55).

CENOZOIC ERA

The two periods of the Cenozoic, the Tertiary and Quaternary, comprise the Age of Mammals, which continues to the present. Grasses became widespread and abundant, and many kinds of large grazing mammals evolved. The Ice Age (see p. 62) was the most recent major geologic event.

MESOZOIC ERA

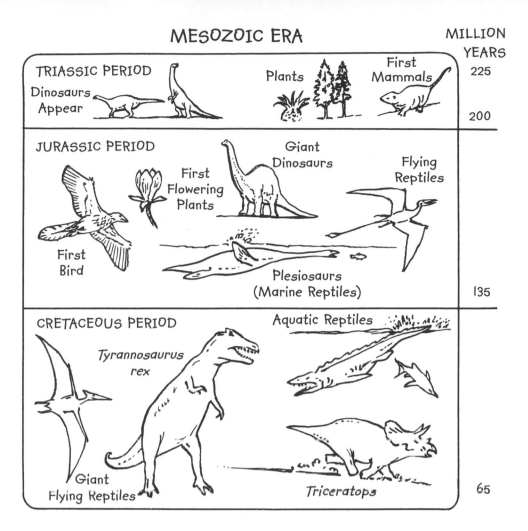

MILLION YEARS

TRIASSIC PERIOD — Dinosaurs Appear — Plants — First Mammals — 225 / 200

JURASSIC PERIOD — First Bird — First Flowering Plants — Giant Dinosaurs — Flying Reptiles — Plesiosaurs (Marine Reptiles) — 135

CRETACEOUS PERIOD — Tyrannosaurus rex — Aquatic Reptiles — Giant Flying Reptiles — Triceratops — 65

CENOZOIC ERA

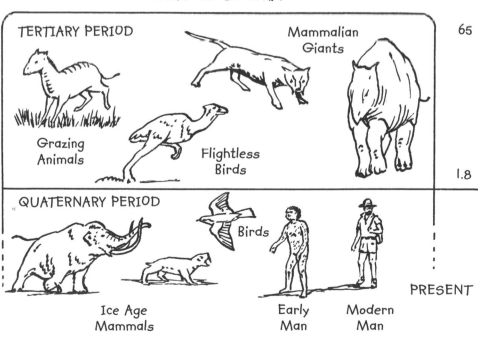

TERTIARY PERIOD — Grazing Animals — Flightless Birds — Mammalian Giants — 65 / 1.8

QUATERNARY PERIOD — Ice Age Mammals — Birds — Early Man — Modern Man — PRESENT

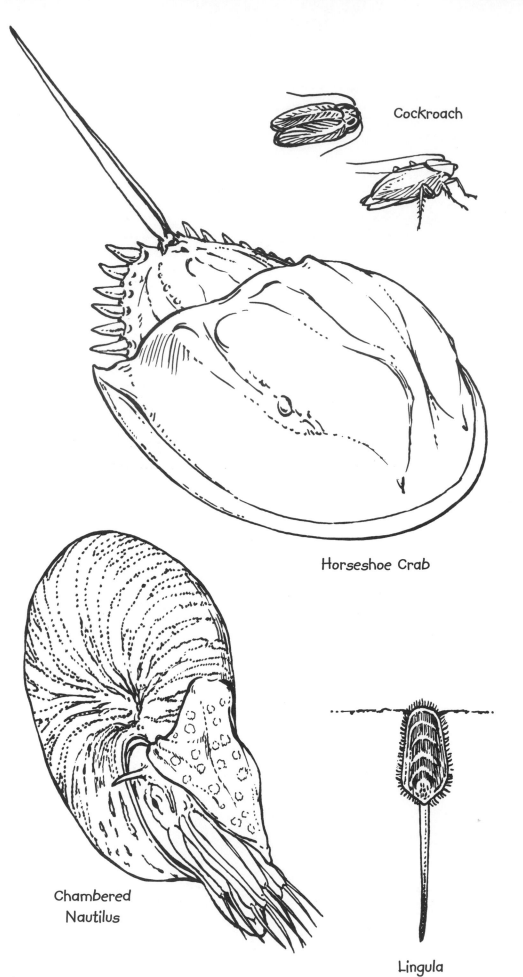

Cockroach

Horseshoe Crab

Chambered
Nautilus

Lingula

LIVING FOSSILS

Some plants and animals that are alive today have long histories traceable in the fossil record of ancient rocks.

Cockroach Cockroaches are among the most common household pests. They date back to the Silurian period, around 400 million years ago. Today there are between 3,000 and 4,000 species. Many have scarcely changed from the time when these nocturnal insects first scurried through primeval undergrowth, long before dinosaurs appeared. (8)

Horseshoe Crab Related to sea scorpions (see p. 9), this common denizen of East Coast seas has barely changed in appearance for 210 million years. Dinosaurs gazed at horseshoe crabs along the seashore, just as beachcombers do today. (9)

Chambered Nautilus Ancestors of this mollusk of deep Pacific waters preyed on the earliest fishes in the Paleozoic. These animals, related to squids, are in the group called cephalopods. The word *cephalopod* means "head-foot," a reference to the many arms in close proximity to their head. Their eyes are very much like our own. (10)

Lingula Most brachiopods (see p. 9) are extinct, but *Lingula* is one of the few exceptions. Its ancestors from the early Paleozoic looked just like it. *Lingula* lives burrowed in the ocean floor, anchored by its long stalk and protected within its clamlike shell. (11)

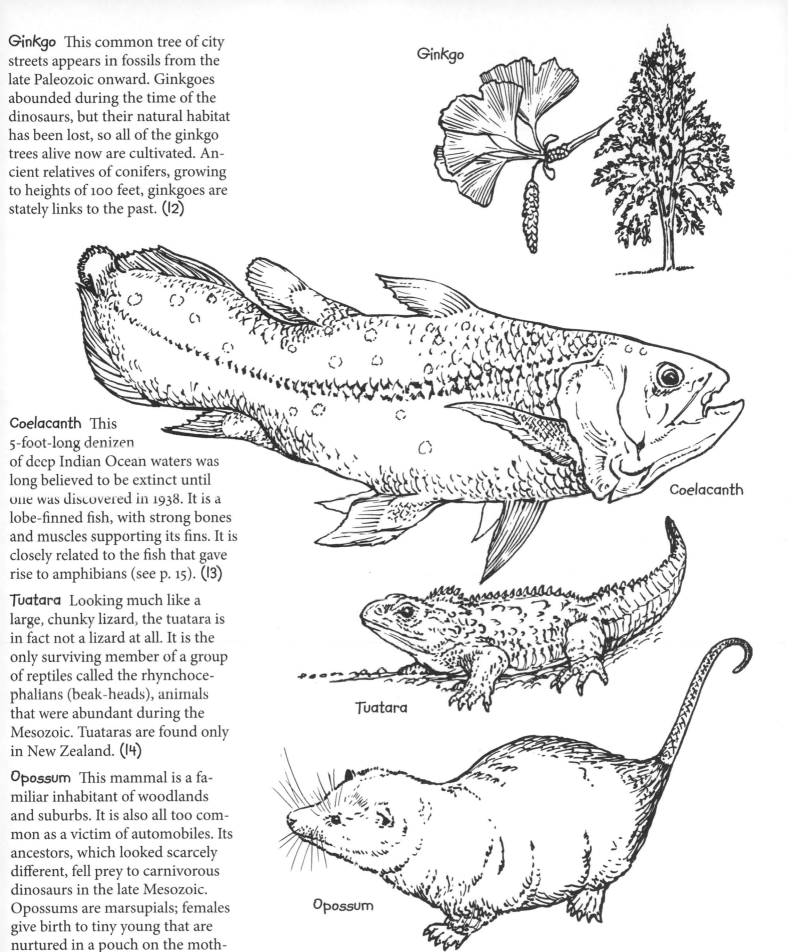

Ginkgo This common tree of city streets appears in fossils from the late Paleozoic onward. Ginkgoes abounded during the time of the dinosaurs, but their natural habitat has been lost, so all of the ginkgo trees alive now are cultivated. Ancient relatives of conifers, growing to heights of 100 feet, ginkgoes are stately links to the past. (12)

Coelacanth This 5-foot-long denizen of deep Indian Ocean waters was long believed to be extinct until one was discovered in 1938. It is a lobe-finned fish, with strong bones and muscles supporting its fins. It is closely related to the fish that gave rise to amphibians (see p. 15). (13)

Tuatara Looking much like a large, chunky lizard, the tuatara is in fact not a lizard at all. It is the only surviving member of a group of reptiles called the rhynchocephalians (beak-heads), animals that were abundant during the Mesozoic. Tuataras are found only in New Zealand. (14)

Opossum This mammal is a familiar inhabitant of woodlands and suburbs. It is also all too common as a victim of automobiles. Its ancestors, which looked scarcely different, fell prey to carnivorous dinosaurs in the late Mesozoic. Opossums are marsupials; females give birth to tiny young that are nurtured in a pouch on the mother's abdomen. (15)

Ginkgo

Coelacanth

Tuatara

Opossum

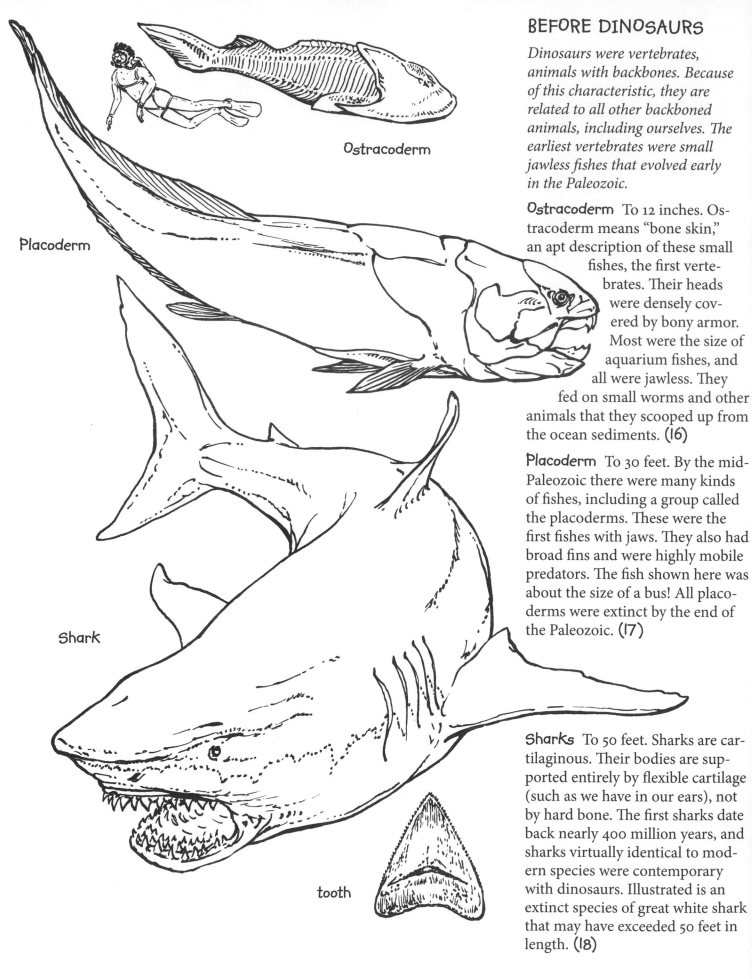

Ostracoderm

Placoderm

Shark

tooth

BEFORE DINOSAURS

Dinosaurs were vertebrates, animals with backbones. Because of this characteristic, they are related to all other backboned animals, including ourselves. The earliest vertebrates were small jawless fishes that evolved early in the Paleozoic.

Ostracoderm To 12 inches. Ostracoderm means "bone skin," an apt description of these small fishes, the first vertebrates. Their heads were densely covered by bony armor. Most were the size of aquarium fishes, and all were jawless. They fed on small worms and other animals that they scooped up from the ocean sediments. (16)

Placoderm To 30 feet. By the mid-Paleozoic there were many kinds of fishes, including a group called the placoderms. These were the first fishes with jaws. They also had broad fins and were highly mobile predators. The fish shown here was about the size of a bus! All placoderms were extinct by the end of the Paleozoic. (17)

Sharks To 50 feet. Sharks are cartilaginous. Their bodies are supported entirely by flexible cartilage (such as we have in our ears), not by hard bone. The first sharks date back nearly 400 million years, and sharks virtually identical to modern species were contemporary with dinosaurs. Illustrated is an extinct species of great white shark that may have exceeded 50 feet in length. (18)

14

Lobe-finned Fishes To 2 feet. These fishes had a bony skeleton and strong bones and muscles supporting their front and hind fins. They could drag themselves over land. They also could gulp and breathe air using a primitive lung. They lived in stagnant ponds and may have moved from pond to pond, breathing air as they did so. Their skull bones and teeth are virtually identical with those of the first amphibians. Lobe-fins lived in the mid-Paleozoic. Their nearest relatives today are the lungfishes and the coelacanth (see p. 13). (19)

Lobe-finned Fishes

Labyrinthodont Amphibian To 6 feet. This bulky, alligator-like amphibian is a far cry from the small, slimy salamanders and frogs of today. It is named for its labyrinth-like tooth structure, which links it to the lobe-finned fishes. Labyrinthodonts thrived during the late Paleozoic era, feeding on other amphibians and fishes. One group gave rise to the stem reptiles. (20)

Labyrinthodont Amphibian

Stem Reptiles To 10 feet. Reptiles have dry skins and lay eggs on land; they do not need water in order to reproduce. Thus reptiles are able to thrive in many landscapes where amphibians cannot survive. The stem reptiles are so called because they gave rise to all other kinds of reptiles, including dinosaurs. Some stem reptiles were only a foot or so in length, but others, like the one shown here, were at least the size of oxen. Their legs sprawled outward, and they probably moved with a waddle. Some were predators, and many, like this one, were plant eaters. (21)

Stem Reptile

LIFE IN THE TRIASSIC PERIOD

The Triassic, which began 225 million years ago, was the first of the three periods of the Mesozoic era. The Paleozoic era ended with the extinction of most land and sea animals, but many new kinds evolved from the survivors to populate the Triassic world. When the Triassic began, all of the major continents were joined together in a massive continent called Pangaea. During the Triassic, Pangaea began to split apart, initially forming two supercontinents: a northern one called Laurasia, which contained what is now North America, Europe, and northern Asia, and a southern one called Gondwanaland, which contained what is now South America, Africa, Antarctica, India, Australia, and parts of southern Asia. This continental drift continues to the present.

The Triassic world was generally cool and dry, and vast deserts covered much of the interior. Forests of cone-bearing trees related to pines and spruces covered the uplands, while along lowland areas grew giant horsetails, ferns, and cycads. Bulky labyrinthodont amphibians still plodded along riverbanks, but reptiles were becoming by far the dominant animals. Crocodile-like phytosaurs inhabited rivers and swamps, along with the first turtles. Swift thecodonts, the ancestors of dinosaurs, scampered along the uplands. Herds of mammal-like reptiles grazed on cycads and horsetails. By the late Triassic the archosaurs had given rise to the first dinosaurs, and herds of plateosaurs roamed the uplands. Some evolutionarily advanced mammal-like reptiles evolved into true mammals, which were to remain small and inconspicuous for another 125 million years.

DINOSAUR ANCESTORS

The ancestors of dinosaurs are called archosaurs. They evolved about 225 million years ago. Most were small, about 3 feet long, and many were aquatic. Some bore striking similarities to crocodiles.

Thecodont To 10 feet. Thecodonts, which thrived during the Triassic period, were ancestors to all dinosaurs. Their name means "teeth in sockets," a characteristic they shared with dinosaurs. Some, like *Euparkeria*, illustrated here, resembled the larger carnivorous dinosaurs that followed. (22)

Phytosaur To 15 feet. Phytosaurs evolved from aquatic thecodonts. They looked almost identical to crocodiles, but their nostrils were located near the eyes at the base of the snout, not at the tip, like crocodile nostrils. Phytosaurs became extinct shortly after crocodiles evolved. The name *phytosaur* means "plant lizard," a misnomer, because they were all carnivores. (23)

Plateosaurus To 20 feet. This was one of the first saurischians, or lizard-hipped dinosaurs. Large herds of these long-necked plant eaters roamed just over 200 million years ago, through what is now Germany and France. Plateosaurs are thought to be ancestral to the huge sauropods and their relatives. Note the anatomical similarity to thecodonts. (24)

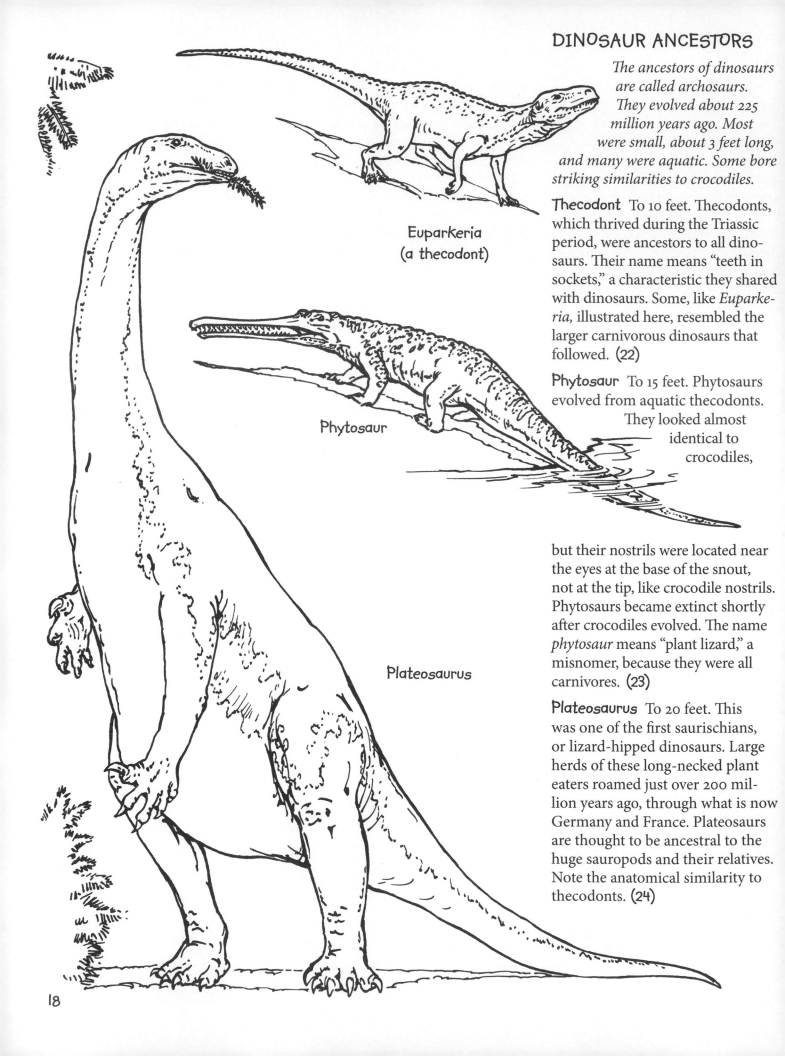

Euparkeria
(a thecodont)

Phytosaur

Plateosaurus

18

COELUROSAURS

The coelurosaurs were a group of small, agile carnivores that are thought to have hunted in packs. They have been called the jackals and hyenas of their time. They evolved in the late Triassic and diversified, persisting through the late Cretaceous. These saurischian dinosaurs were rather like miniature, streamlined tyrannosaurs. Most had long necks and tails, with forelimbs that were useful for

Coelophysis

grasping. Coelurosaurs ranged in size from 2 feet to 18 feet.

Coelophysis To 10 feet. This 65-pound dinosaur was the wolf of the late Triassic. Its teeth were sharp and serrated, and it may have hunted in small groups. In a remote place in New Mexico called Ghost Ranch, numerous skeletons of adults and young have been excavated. There is also evidence that some of the adults may have killed and eaten some of the young. (25)

Compsognathus To 2 feet. One of the smallest dinosaurs (barely the size of a chicken), tiny *Compsognathus* must have pursued insects and very small vertebrates. It also may have eaten eggs. Some scientists believe it may have been warm-blooded (see p. 7). Perhaps it was covered with feathers or hairlike insulation. (26)

Compsognathus

THE HUGE SAUROPODS

"Thunder lizard" is an apt name for the sauropods, the huge plant eaters of the Jurassic period and, to a lesser extent, the Cretaceous period. Some of these dinosaurs would dwarf the largest elephant. They probably lived in herds, foraging on needles from tall conifers that they reached with their long necks. When sauropods were first discovered, it was believed that they were too large to stand on land. This belief gave rise to the notion that they lived in swamps and lakes, where their bulk could be buoyed, or held up, by water. Though these dinosaurs may have cooled their bodies by soaking in lakes, their body structure was more than adequate to support their weight on land. They probably moved quite efficiently, much as modern elephants do.

Apatosaurus To 70 feet. This dinosaur was formerly named *Brontosaurus,* which means "thunder lizard." It probably tipped the scales at about 36 tons! (An elephant weighs 3 to 6 tons.) This is one of the best-known dinosaurs. Its remains have been found both in Europe and in the western United States. Like all large sauropods, *Apatosaurus's* head was small in relation to its body size. It probably fed by swallowing

Apatosaurus

large quantities of vegetation and grinding it up in a gizzardlike stomach. (27)

Diplodocus To 90 feet. This sauropod is a slender version of *Apatosaurus*, to which it was closely related. *Diplodocus*'s neck measured 26 feet and its tail 45 feet, but it probably weighed "only" 12 tons. It may have used its powerful whip-like tail as a defense against large predatory dinosaurs. Its head was somewhat elongated, with peglike teeth suitable for snipping vegeta-

Diplodocus

tion but not for grinding. *Diplodocus* roamed the area now known as the western United States during the Jurassic. (28)

Camarasaurus To 60 feet. This husky sauropod inhabited what is now Colorado and Utah during the Jurassic period. Its neck and tail were proportionately shorter than those of *Apatosaurus* and *Diplodocus*. The odd position of its nostrils, high on the skull, suggested to some scientists that this dinosaur had a trunk. Most scientists now think that the large nostrils could have been highly sensitive to odors or may have been used to cool the blood. *Diplodocus*'s teeth were chisel-like and very close together. This creature probably ate very coarse, tough plants. (29)

Camarasaurus

21

Brachiosaurus To 80 feet. The brachiosaurs, which ranged widely over Europe, Africa, and North America during the late Jurassic and early Cretaceous periods, had the most massive bodies of any dinosaurs. An adult *Brachiosaurus* weighed about 66 tons! From toes to nostrils, the animal was 40 feet in height. Unlike most sauropods, brachiosaurs had longer forelegs than hind legs, adding to their overall height (the name means "arm-lizard"). Nostrils were positioned high atop the skull, leading some to suggest that they served as snorkels, allowing the huge animal to breathe while submerged. This could not be true, because if the dinosaur had its entire body below the water's surface, the water pressure at that depth would prevent it from expanding its chest to breathe! Like other sauropods, brachiosaurs probably fed on leaves cropped from tall trees, much as modern (but much smaller) giraffes do. (30)

Fossils found in the western United States suggest that creatures similar to but even larger than *Brachiosaurus* existed. One, called *Supersaurus,* may have had a head 54 feet above the ground. Another, called *Ultrosaurus,* may have weighed 150 tons, with a length of more than 100 feet. Such huge dinosaurs would be tall enough to look into a six-story building, and would have eaten 5 tons of plant food per day!

Brachiosaurus

THEROPOD CARNOSAURS

Theropods are one of the two groups of saurischians, or lizard-hipped dinosaurs. Carnosaurs, one of the major kinds of theropods, were the lions and tigers of the dinosaur world. These bipedal (two-legged), often large dinosaurs were all meat eaters. Their body structure suggests that they pursued their prey by running on their strong hind legs, with their bodies held nearly horizontal and their stiff tails extended behind for balance. Their small forelimbs were probably used to tear apart prey after the kill. Carnosaurs had large skulls lined with sharp, often serrated teeth, ideal for killing and ripping apart flesh.

Dilophosaurus To 20 feet. This carnosaur is notable both for the odd double crest atop its head and for its jaw structure, which was much weaker than that of most carnosaurs. It lived early in the Jurassic, long before the allosaurs evolved. **(31)**

Allosaurus To 39 feet. Perhaps the largest carnosaur of the Jurassic period, a mature *Allosaurus* could weigh up to 4 tons. Its fearsome head was held 15 feet above the ground. It probably hunted brontosaurs, killing them with teeth serrated on both sides and housed in a skull that measured a yard in length! It lived in the area now covered by the western United States. **(32)**

Ceratosaurus To 20 feet. Unusual among carnosaurs for the odd hornlike projection on its nose, *Ceratosaurus* lived in North America during the late Jurassic period. **(33)**

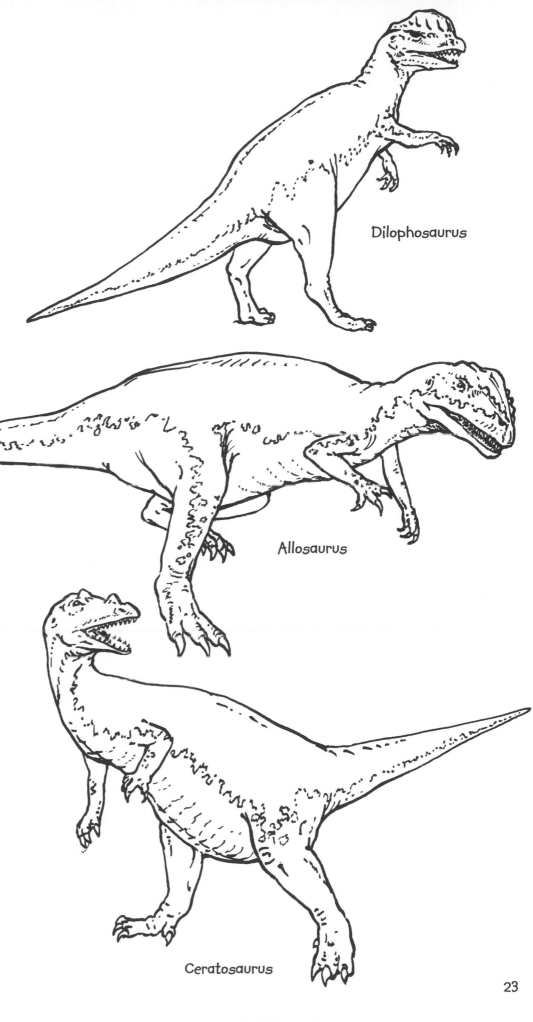

Dilophosaurus

Allosaurus

Ceratosaurus

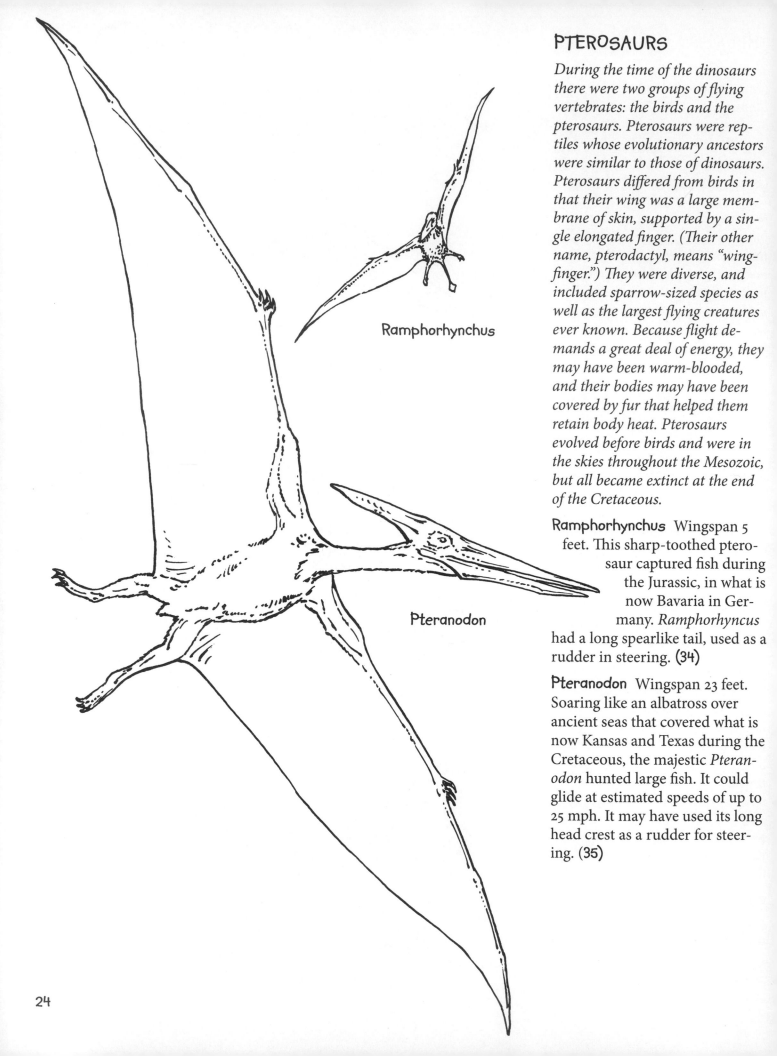

Ramphorhynchus

Pteranodon

PTEROSAURS

During the time of the dinosaurs there were two groups of flying vertebrates: the birds and the pterosaurs. Pterosaurs were reptiles whose evolutionary ancestors were similar to those of dinosaurs. Pterosaurs differed from birds in that their wing was a large membrane of skin, supported by a single elongated finger. (Their other name, pterodactyl, means "wing-finger.") They were diverse, and included sparrow-sized species as well as the largest flying creatures ever known. Because flight demands a great deal of energy, they may have been warm-blooded, and their bodies may have been covered by fur that helped them retain body heat. Pterosaurs evolved before birds and were in the skies throughout the Mesozoic, but all became extinct at the end of the Cretaceous.

Ramphorhynchus Wingspan 5 feet. This sharp-toothed pterosaur captured fish during the Jurassic, in what is now Bavaria in Germany. *Ramphorhyncus* had a long spearlike tail, used as a rudder in steering. (34)

Pteranodon Wingspan 23 feet. Soaring like an albatross over ancient seas that covered what is now Kansas and Texas during the Cretaceous, the majestic *Pteranodon* hunted large fish. It could glide at estimated speeds of up to 25 mph. It may have used its long head crest as a rudder for steering. (35)

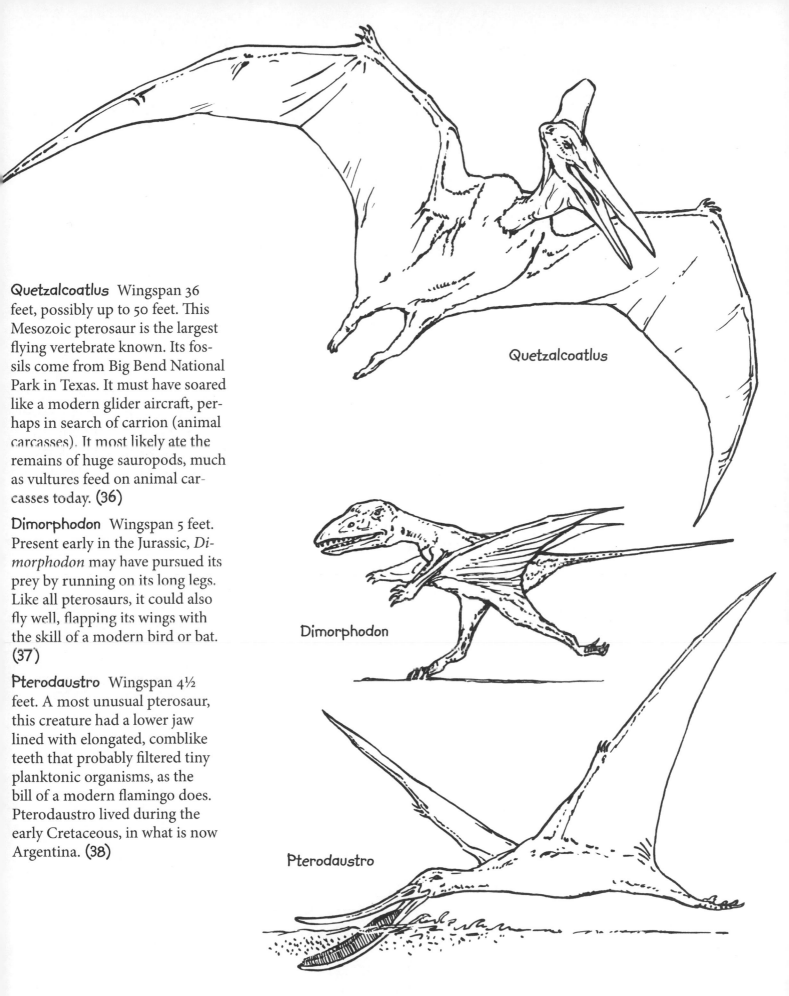

Quetzalcoatlus Wingspan 36 feet, possibly up to 50 feet. This Mesozoic pterosaur is the largest flying vertebrate known. Its fossils come from Big Bend National Park in Texas. It must have soared like a modern glider aircraft, perhaps in search of carrion (animal carcasses). It most likely ate the remains of huge sauropods, much as vultures feed on animal carcasses today. **(36)**

Dimorphodon Wingspan 5 feet. Present early in the Jurassic, *Dimorphodon* may have pursued its prey by running on its long legs. Like all pterosaurs, it could also fly well, flapping its wings with the skill of a modern bird or bat. **(37)**

Pterodaustro Wingspan 4½ feet. A most unusual pterosaur, this creature had a lower jaw lined with elongated, comblike teeth that probably filtered tiny planktonic organisms, as the bill of a modern flamingo does. Pterodaustro lived during the early Cretaceous, in what is now Argentina. **(38)**

Quetzalcoatlus

Dimorphodon

Pterodaustro

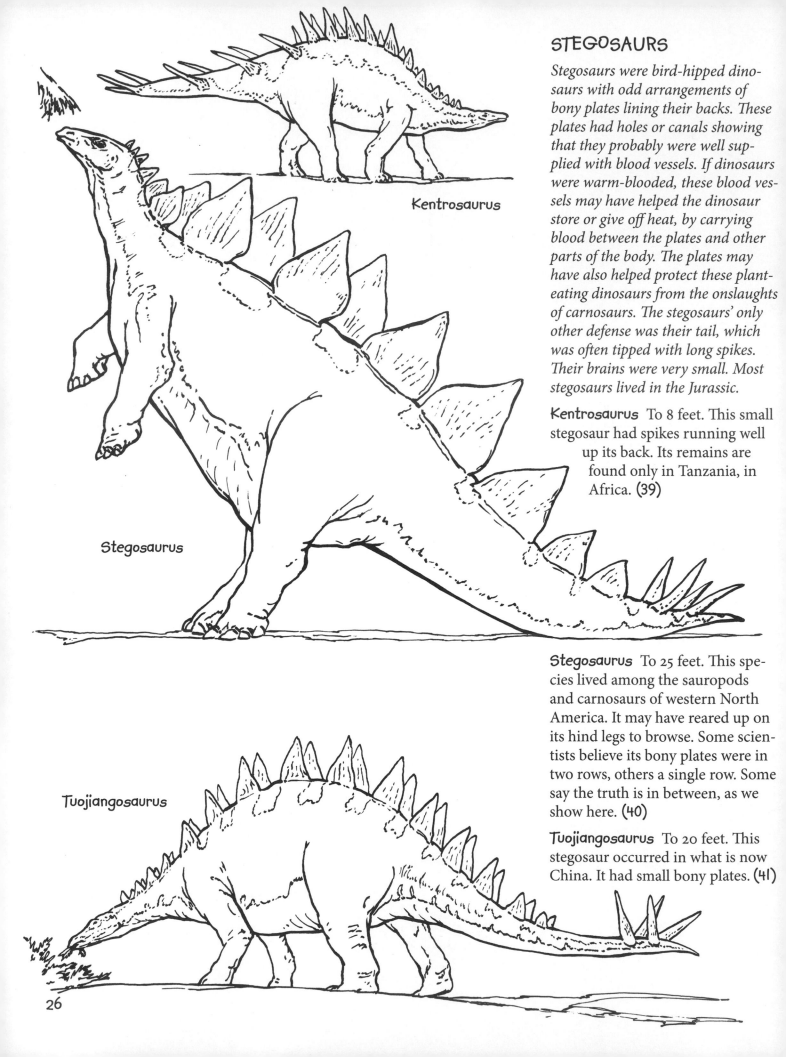

STEGOSAURS

Stegosaurs were bird-hipped dinosaurs with odd arrangements of bony plates lining their backs. These plates had holes or canals showing that they probably were well supplied with blood vessels. If dinosaurs were warm-blooded, these blood vessels may have helped the dinosaur store or give off heat, by carrying blood between the plates and other parts of the body. The plates may have also helped protect these plant-eating dinosaurs from the onslaughts of carnosaurs. The stegosaurs' only other defense was their tail, which was often tipped with long spikes. Their brains were very small. Most stegosaurs lived in the Jurassic.

Kentrosaurus To 8 feet. This small stegosaur had spikes running well up its back. Its remains are found only in Tanzania, in Africa. **(39)**

Stegosaurus To 25 feet. This species lived among the sauropods and carnosaurs of western North America. It may have reared up on its hind legs to browse. Some scientists believe its bony plates were in two rows, others a single row. Some say the truth is in between, as we show here. **(40)**

Tuojiangosaurus To 20 feet. This stegosaur occurred in what is now China. It had small bony plates. **(41)**

Kentrosaurus

Stegosaurus

Tuojiangosaurus

Megalosaurus To 30 feet. This carnosaur of the mid-Jurassic period was one of the first fossilized dinosaurs to be discovered. A description of the very first dinosaur discovered — *Iguanodon* (see p. 49) — was published in 1822, and the world was informed of *Megalosaurus* in 1824. The original fossil, which consisted only of a part of the lower jawbone (with teeth), came from Oxford, England. The teeth were so impressively large that the total length of the animal was estimated at first to be 40 feet, but more complete specimens later revealed that it was actually 10 feet shorter. The earliest restorations include an impressive full-scale sculpture that can still be seen in south London on the grounds of the old Crystal Palace, built for the Great Exhibition of 1851, during the reign of Queen Victoria. In this restoration the animal looks rather like a rhinoceros, walking on all fours. Only later, when far more complete skeletons were unearthed, was the true shape realized. (42)

Megalosaurus skeletons have been found in the United States, Australia, Europe, Africa, and India. Such a wide distribution provides support for the belief that the continents were tightly connected during the Jurassic period. Certainly these land-dwelling dinosaurs could never have crossed oceans to reach all of these scattered continents if these landmasses had been in their present positions.

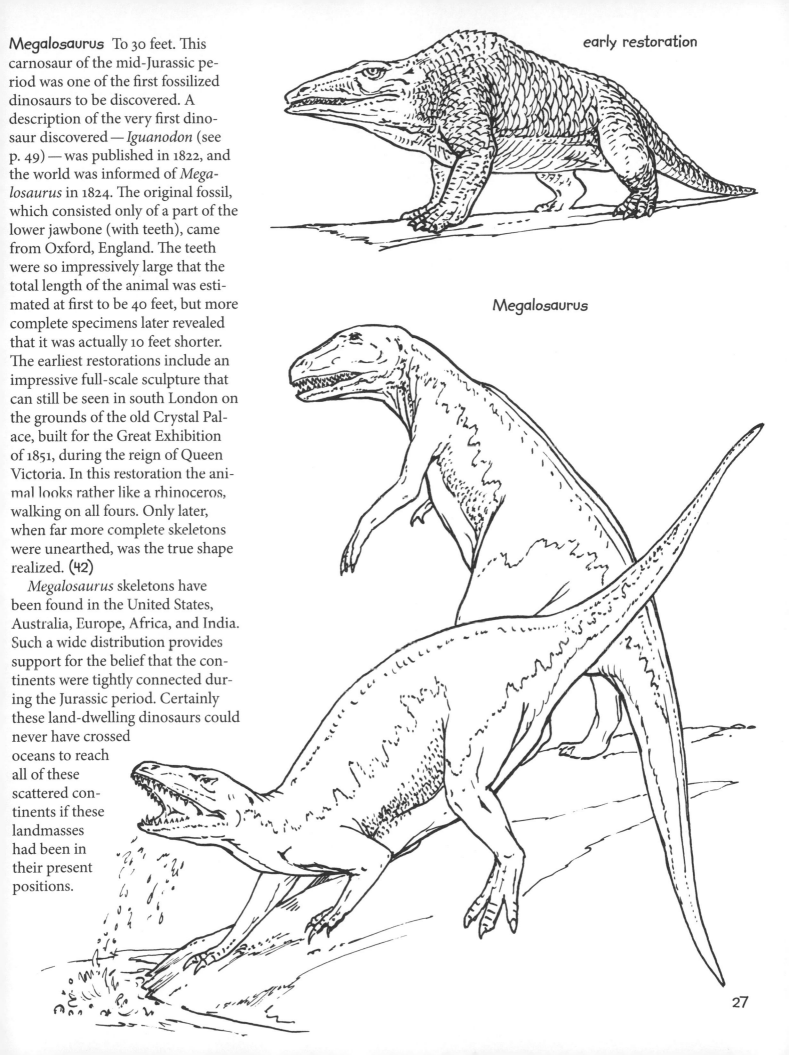

early restoration

Megalosaurus

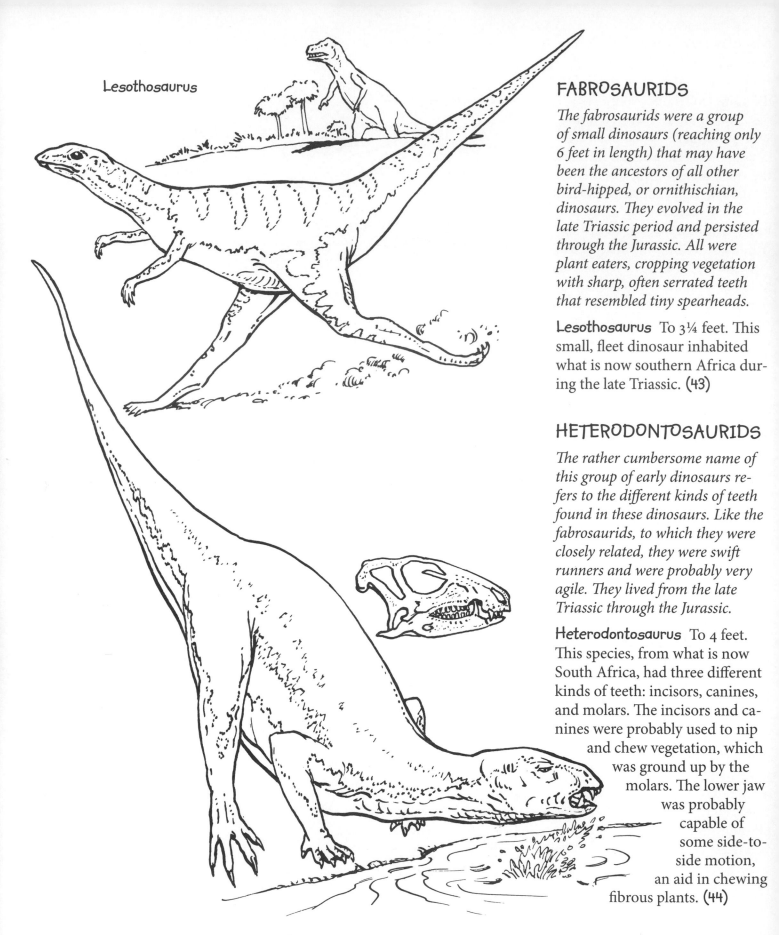

Lesothosaurus

FABROSAURIDS

The fabrosaurids were a group of small dinosaurs (reaching only 6 feet in length) that may have been the ancestors of all other bird-hipped, or ornithischian, dinosaurs. They evolved in the late Triassic period and persisted through the Jurassic. All were plant eaters, cropping vegetation with sharp, often serrated teeth that resembled tiny spearheads.

Lesothosaurus To 3¼ feet. This small, fleet dinosaur inhabited what is now southern Africa during the late Triassic. (43)

HETERODONTOSAURIDS

The rather cumbersome name of this group of early dinosaurs refers to the different kinds of teeth found in these dinosaurs. Like the fabrosaurids, to which they were closely related, they were swift runners and were probably very agile. They lived from the late Triassic through the Jurassic.

Heterodontosaurus To 4 feet. This species, from what is now South Africa, had three different kinds of teeth: incisors, canines, and molars. The incisors and canines were probably used to nip and chew vegetation, which was ground up by the molars. The lower jaw was probably capable of some side-to-side motion, an aid in chewing fibrous plants. (44)

Heterodontosaurus

AN UNUSUAL SAUROPOD

Saltasaurus To 39 feet. Many people believe that most dinosaurs have been discovered and their fossils excavated. However, part of the excitement that surrounds the study of dinosaurs is that new kinds are still being unearthed, and some of these animals are indeed unique. Such is the case with *Saltasaurus*. This rather small sauropod is named for the area in Argentina where it was discovered in 1980. Though it was a rather husky sauropod, *Saltasaurus* bones were found along with remains of what must have been skin armor. Apparently this dinosaur was protected by thick, oval, bony plates scattered among a dense covering of hardened studs that projected outward, perhaps resembling the skin of a crocodile. The skeleton of *Saltasaurus* indicates that, like all sauropods, this dinosaur was quite strong but also rather agile. *Saltasaurus* had a strengthened tail and probably could have stood on its hind legs, using its tail as a prop as a kangaroo does. This maneuver would help the animal reach tall vegetation. *Saltasaurus* was one of the last of the dinosaurs; it lived in the late Cretaceous period. (45)

Saltasaurus

LIFE IN THE JURASSIC PERIOD

Throughout the 57 million years of the Jurassic period, dinosaurs were the dominant land animals. Much of the world's climate was tropical, warm, and humid, and upland coniferous forests were interspersed with giant horsetail forests in lowland swamps. The continents continued to drift. North America and Europe began to separate, forming the new Atlantic Ocean. Gondwanaland was also breaking apart: South America and Africa separated, India moved northward, Antarctica began drifting toward the South Pole, and Australia moved eastward. Bird-hipped dinosaurs, including the camptosaurs (see p. 32) and plate-backed stegosaurs, were abundant and, along with equally abundant herds of immense lizard-hipped sauropod dinosaurs, fed on varieties of conifers, cycads, and a group of plants called bennettitaleans that resembled palms. Large carnosaurs, among them *Allosaurus* and *Ceratosaurus,* stalked the massive plant eaters. Ichthyosaurs and plesiosaurs snapped up fishes in the oceans, as crocodiles did in rivers and swamps. The flying pterosaurs diversified and soon shared the skies with true birds, for it was during the Jurassic that *Archaeopteryx* (see p. 40) evolved from small coelurosaur dinosaurs. The steamy Jurassic was ruled by the giant reptiles. Mammals continued to evolve but remained small and inconspicuous.

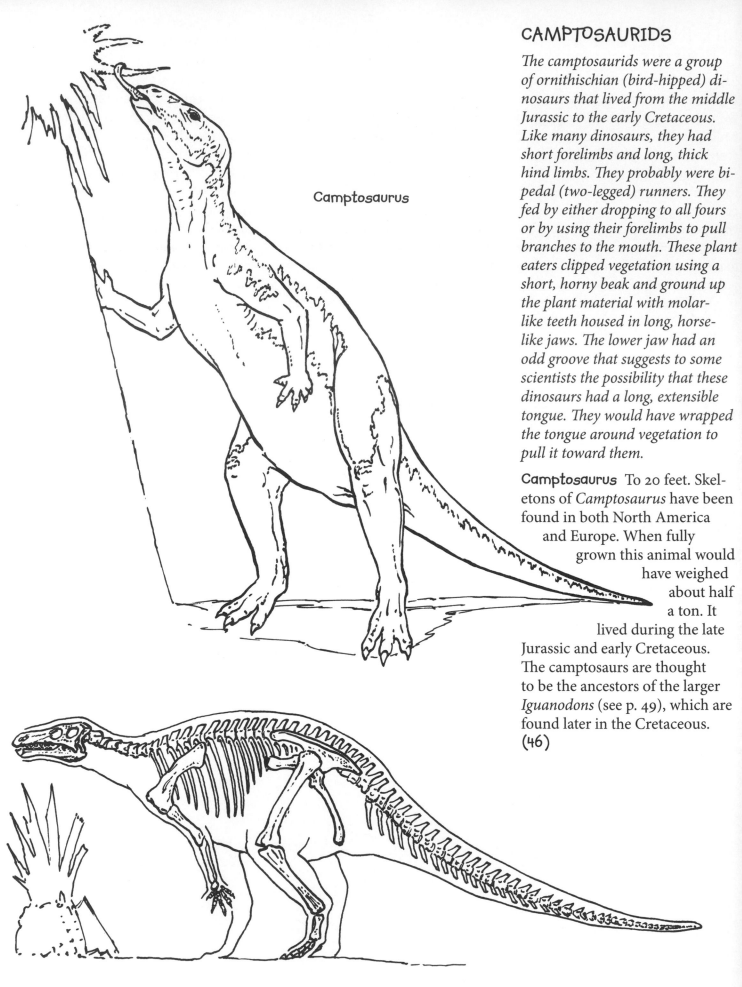

Camptosaurus

CAMPTOSAURIDS

The camptosaurids were a group of ornithischian (bird-hipped) dinosaurs that lived from the middle Jurassic to the early Cretaceous. Like many dinosaurs, they had short forelimbs and long, thick hind limbs. They probably were bipedal (two-legged) runners. They fed by either dropping to all fours or by using their forelimbs to pull branches to the mouth. These plant eaters clipped vegetation using a short, horny beak and ground up the plant material with molar-like teeth housed in long, horse-like jaws. The lower jaw had an odd groove that suggests to some scientists the possibility that these dinosaurs had a long, extensible tongue. They would have wrapped the tongue around vegetation to pull it toward them.

Camptosaurus To 20 feet. Skeletons of *Camptosaurus* have been found in both North America and Europe. When fully grown this animal would have weighed about half a ton. It lived during the late Jurassic and early Cretaceous. The camptosaurs are thought to be the ancestors of the larger *Iguanodons* (see p. 49), which are found later in the Cretaceous. (46)

HYPSILOPHODONTIDS

Appearing first in the mid-Jurassic period and lasting through the Cretaceous, the hypsilophodontids were a diverse and successful group of plant eaters. They were ornithischians, similar in many respects to fabrosaurids (see p. 28), and were small dinosaurs, ranging in length from about 6 feet to 16 feet. Their skulls and teeth were well structured for chewing coarse vegetation, and their jaw muscles were powerful. Their teeth were long, close together, and suited for grinding. A horny beak, probably helpful in cropping plants, covered the tip of the upper jaw.

These dinosaurs have been called the gazelles of their time. They had long legs, including an elongated ankle and foot, and could run very swiftly. The tail was stiffly supported by tendons, and acted as a counterbalance as the animal ran.

Hypsilophodon To 7½ feet. This dinosaur lived in the early Cretaceous and ranged widely — specimens have been found from North Dakota to England. Its anatomy indicates that it must have been a very swift runner, though early reconstructions mistakenly showed it as a tree dweller! (47)

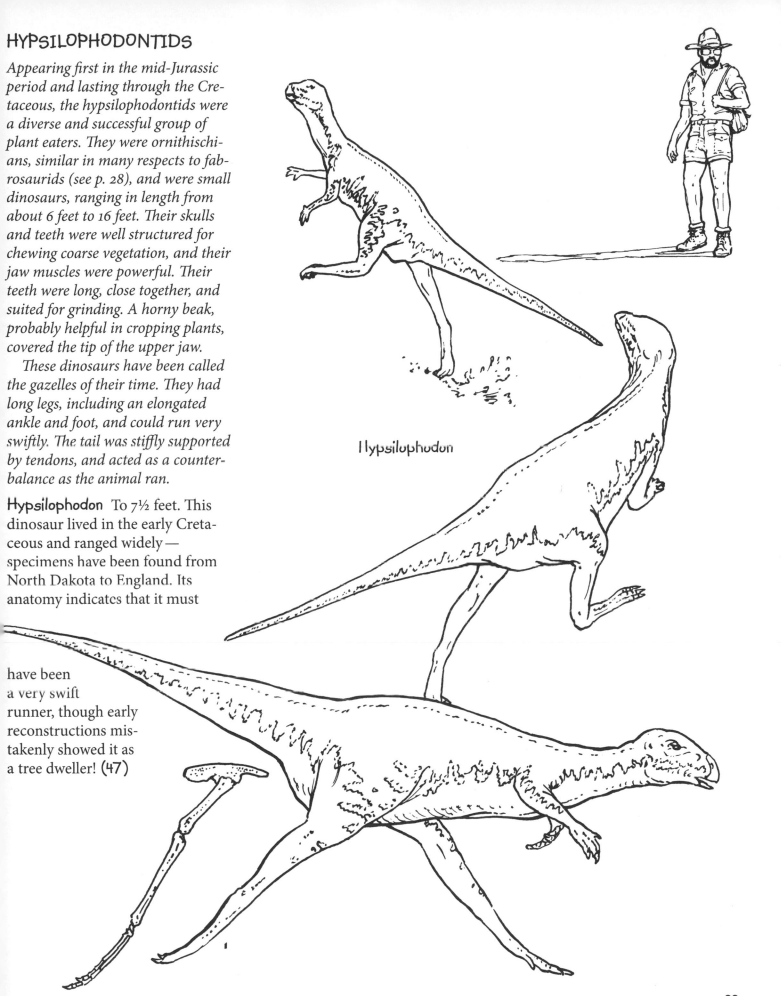

Hypsilophodon

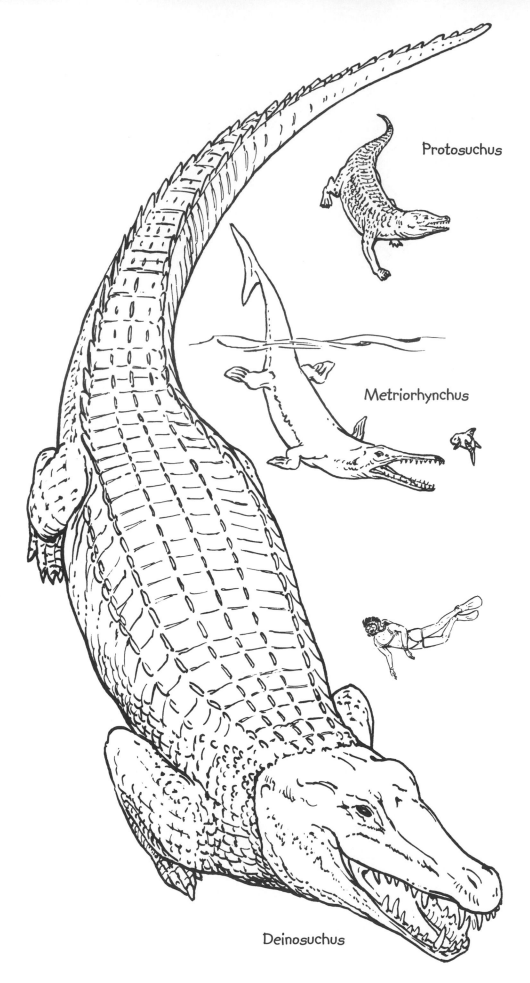

Protosuchus

Metriorhynchus

Deinosuchus

CROCODILIANS

Crocodiles and alligators are considered "modern" reptiles because they are still with us. However, as a group, the crocodilians have existed since the Triassic. The largest crocodiles ever to exist lived at the same time as the dinosaurs. Crocodilians are most definitely not dinosaurs, though they do share a common thecodont ancestor (see p. 18). Crocodiles have changed little over their millions of years on the planet. All are aquatic carnivores, with powerful tails used in swimming and long jaws armed with sharp teeth.

Protosuchus To 3½ feet. This little animal was one of the first crocodilians. Its fossils have been found in the American Southwest and date from the late Triassic period. *Protosuchus* had longer legs and a shorter skull than modern crocodiles. Like modern members of its group, it had thickened skin protecting its back. **(48)**

Metriorhynchus To 10 feet. This crocodile was unusual because it had paddle-like flippers rather than legs, and a whale-like tail. These characteristics indicate that it was totally aquatic. It probably pursued fishes, which it captured with its slender, tooth-laden snout. Another unusual feature was the total lack of armor on the skin. *Metriorhynchus* lived in the Jurassic period. **(49)**

Deinosuchus To 50 feet. Imagine a crocodile so long that it extends almost from the pitcher's mound to home plate! This immense animal, the largest crocodile known, lived during the late Cretaceous period. It was quite capable of devouring dinosaurs, perhaps grabbing them as they came to the water's edge to drink. Fossils come from Texas, a state known for bigness. **(50)**

LIZARDS, SNAKES, AND TURTLES

Besides crocodilians, there are three other major reptile groups alive today. Each group traces its roots back to the Mesozoic era. Lizards evolved in the latter part of the Triassic and are thriving today: there are about 6,000 species, mostly in warm regions such as rain forests and deserts. Snakes first appear in the fossil record from the late Cretaceous. In many respects they are similar to lizards, though they lack limbs. The most ancient snakes are the huge constrictors, whose modern species include the pythons and the Anaconda. Turtles date back to the Triassic. They differ from both dinosaurs and other modern reptiles in that their ancestor is not a thecodont (see p. 18). Turtles evolved from a very early group of reptiles before the Mesozoic began.

Archelon To 12 feet. *Archelon* was a large sea turtle of the Cretaceous period. It lived in a vast inland sea covering what is now South Dakota, where its fossils were found. The name means "ruler turtle," a reference to its large size. (51)

Mosasaur To 30 feet. Mosasaurs were large aquatic lizards of the Cretaceous. *Tylosaurus,* shown here, lived in a sea that covered Kansas 70 million years ago. The paddle-like feet and long tail made mosasaurs efficient swimmers. (52)

Python To 30 feet or more. These thick-bodied snakes kill their prey by constriction, preventing their victims from breathing. The reticulated python, shown here, is alive today, found in Southeast Asia. It can reach a length of 33 feet. Fossil pythons appear to be quite similar. (53)

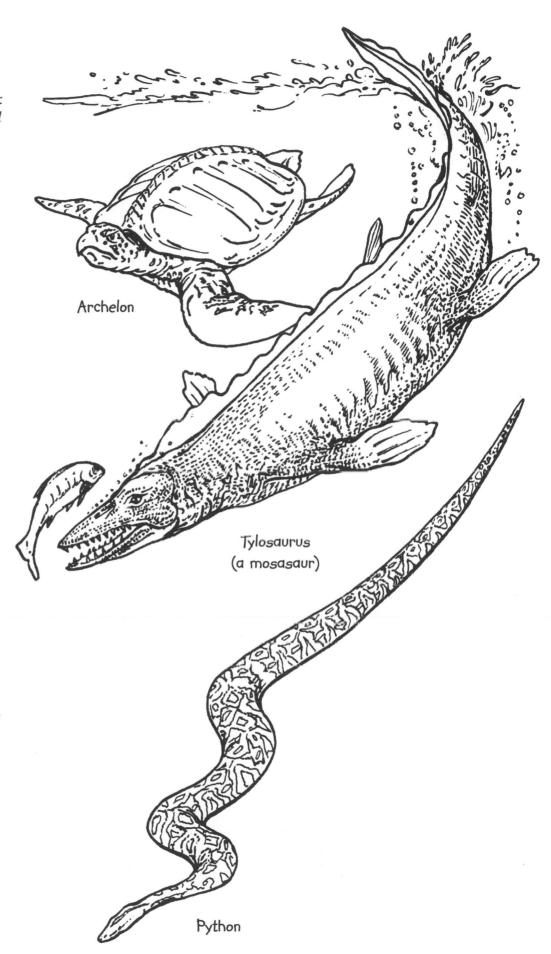

Archelon

Tylosaurus
(a mosasaur)

Python

LIFE IN THE CRETACEOUS PERIOD

During the 71-million-year span of the Cretaceous period the great mountain ranges of the Rockies and Andes formed. A map of the Cretaceous world would show an arrangement of continents similar to that of the present day. Dinosaurs continued to thrive into the mid-Cretaceous but then began to decline, becoming totally extinct by the close of the period 65 million years ago (see pp. 54–55). Among the dinosaurs appeared the bulky ankylosaurs (see p. 43) and ceratopsids, both pursued by the huge and ferocious tyrannosaurs. Duck-billed dinosaurs, among them the many kinds of crested hadrosaurs (see p. 50), roamed in vast herds along with various long-necked sauro-

pods, grazing on many kinds of trees. Ginkgoes and pines were abundant, and familiar trees such as the oaks, magnolias, hickories, dogwoods, and sassafrases appeared. The leaves of these trees were an important source of food for dinosaur herds. Many new species of flowering plants produced pollen that was fed upon by new kinds of insects, among them bees and butterflies. As these insects visited various plants, they helped cross-pollinate the plants, just as bees and other insects do today. Tall, dark forests of giant sequoias and redwoods sheltered ostrich dinosaurs and *Iguanodons* as packs of *Deinonychus* hunted them.

The first grasses appeared, adding meadows to the Cretaceous scene. Seas were homes of huge sea serpents, the plesiosaurs, as well as fishlike ichthyosaurs (see p. 45) and giant mosasaur lizards. Bony fishes, much like those alive today, swam with sharks and giant turtles. Overhead flew the largest of the pterosaurs, as well as various ancient birds. Though still inconspicuous, mammals were lurking in the underbrush, some closely resembling modern opossums. The world was soon to be theirs, when the great dinosaurs became extinct.

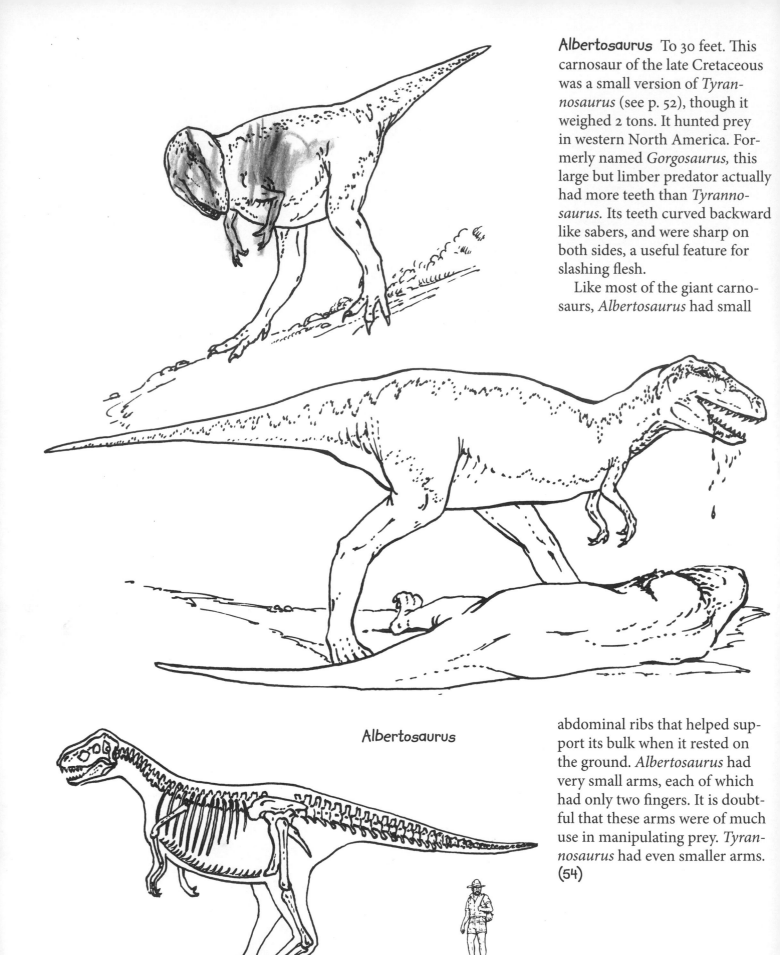

Albertosaurus To 30 feet. This carnosaur of the late Cretaceous was a small version of *Tyrannosaurus* (see p. 52), though it weighed 2 tons. It hunted prey in western North America. Formerly named *Gorgosaurus*, this large but limber predator actually had more teeth than *Tyrannosaurus*. Its teeth curved backward like sabers, and were sharp on both sides, a useful feature for slashing flesh.

Like most of the giant carnosaurs, *Albertosaurus* had small

Albertosaurus

abdominal ribs that helped support its bulk when it rested on the ground. *Albertosaurus* had very small arms, each of which had only two fingers. It is doubtful that these arms were of much use in manipulating prey. *Tyrannosaurus* had even smaller arms. (54)

BONE-HEADED DINOSAURS

In the late Cretaceous period there lived an odd group of plant-eating dinosaurs with very dense bony skulls, raised in a dome-like shape. It is not clear exactly which major group of dinosaurs gave rise to the bone-heads. Some believe they should be classified as ornithopods (see p. 49), while others believe they should be in their own group.

Pachycephalosaurus To 25 feet. The rather cumbersome name of this dinosaur means "thick-headed lizard." It is well named, considering that its domed skull was a 9-inch-thick layer of bone surrounding the tiny brain. The nose and rear of the skull were covered by odd bumps and bony nodules. Many experts now believe that these bone-heads used their thick skulls in butting contests, much as bighorn sheep do today. Perhaps the males established their dominance by out-butting their rivals. (55)

Stegoceras To 6 feet. Enough fossils of this small bone-head have been discovered to allow scientists to trace how the domed, thick skull grew. Males may have had thicker skulls than females, and juveniles (young) had much less bony skulls. The backbone and tail were reinforced by tendons, which helped the animal keep its balance as it used its head as a battering ram. (56)

Pachycephalosaurus

Stegoceras

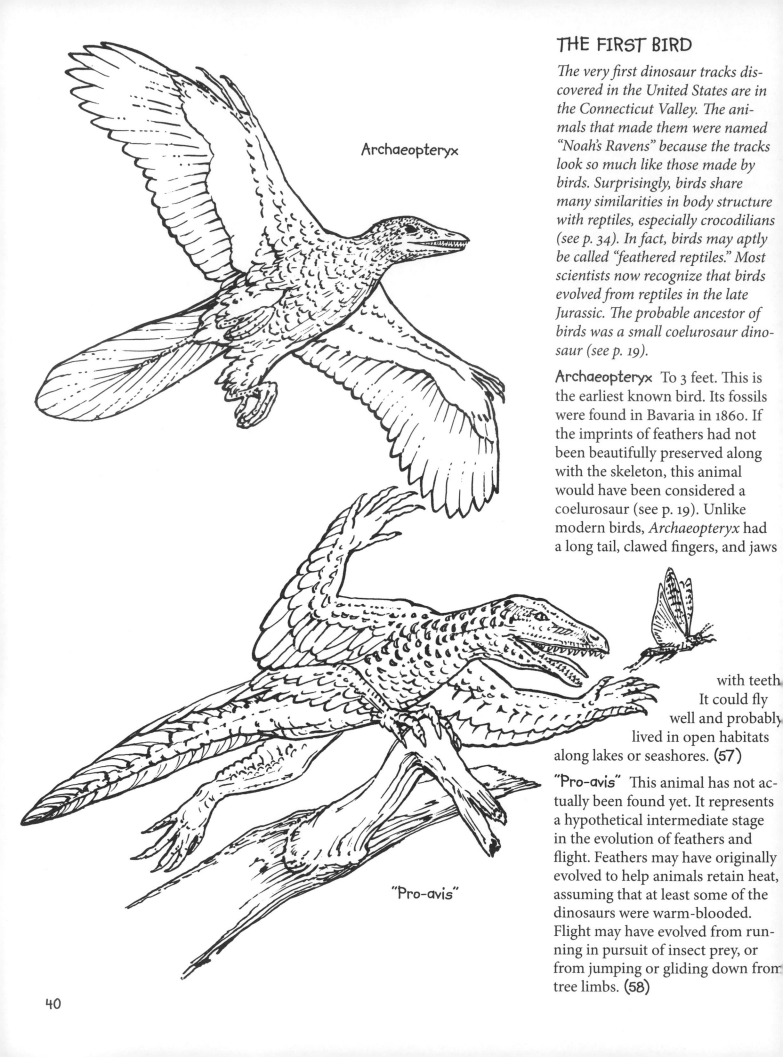

Archaeopteryx

"Pro-avis"

THE FIRST BIRD

The very first dinosaur tracks discovered in the United States are in the Connecticut Valley. The animals that made them were named "Noah's Ravens" because the tracks look so much like those made by birds. Surprisingly, birds share many similarities in body structure with reptiles, especially crocodilians (see p. 34). In fact, birds may aptly be called "feathered reptiles." Most scientists now recognize that birds evolved from reptiles in the late Jurassic. The probable ancestor of birds was a small coelurosaur dinosaur (see p. 19).

Archaeopteryx To 3 feet. This is the earliest known bird. Its fossils were found in Bavaria in 1860. If the imprints of feathers had not been beautifully preserved along with the skeleton, this animal would have been considered a coelurosaur (see p. 19). Unlike modern birds, *Archaeopteryx* had a long tail, clawed fingers, and jaws with teeth. It could fly well and probably lived in open habitats along lakes or seashores. **(57)**

"Pro-avis" This animal has not actually been found yet. It represents a hypothetical intermediate stage in the evolution of feathers and flight. Feathers may have originally evolved to help animals retain heat, assuming that at least some of the dinosaurs were warm-blooded. Flight may have evolved from running in pursuit of insect prey, or from jumping or gliding down from tree limbs. **(58)**

OSTRICH DINOSAURS

As the name implies, these dinosaurs of the late Cretaceous period bore a resemblance to ostriches. Related to the coelurosaurs (see p. 19), they were slender, swift

carnivores that probably fed on insects, mammals, baby dinosaurs, and dinosaur eggs.

Struthiomimus To 12 feet in length. This dinosaur, whose name means "ostrich mimic," looked like a modern ostrich without feathers. Its long, strong hind legs made it capable of running at great speed. Its arms were also long, with three fingers that were probably useful for manipulating small prey. Its eyes were large, and its jaws lacked teeth, making the skull quite birdlike in appearance. The dinosaur stood about 6 feet tall. **(59)**

One strange fossil found in Mongolia is named *Deinocheirus*, which means "terrible claw." It may have been a gigantic ostrich dinosaur. Only the arms were found. Each has three huge slashing claws, and each arm measures 8½ feet long!

Oviraptor To 6 feet. This little dinosaur's name means "egg stealer." The first fossils were found in Outer Mongolia near the nests of *Protoceratops* (see p. 47). This led some scientists to speculate that *Oviraptor* was killed in a sandstorm while in the act of stealing eggs. This dinosaur's skull lacked teeth but may have been covered by a horny sheath. **(60)**

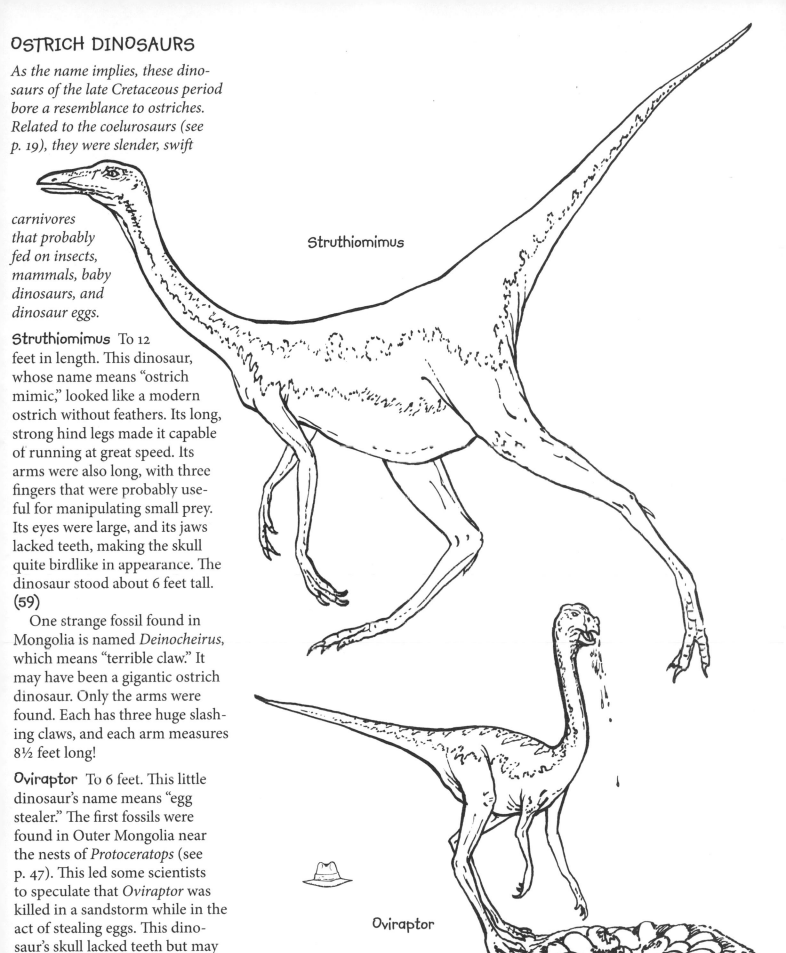

Struthiomimus

Oviraptor

Deinonychus To 10 feet. This small dinosaur from western North America was first described in 1969. The name *Deinonychus* means "terrible claw," a reference to the large curved claw on the second toe of the hind foot. This claw was jointed, which would have allowed it to be raised and lowered efficiently. It probably was held aboveground as the animal ran and was used for slashing, to bring down and dismember prey. *Deinonychus* was probably an effective little predator that hunted in packs, like modern wolves. Though each one weighed only about 150 pounds and was barely 5 feet tall, a pack of these swift dinosaurs could have been more than a match for a large sauropod. Their hind legs were long and strong, ideal for running. Their tails were rigid, supported by tendons that added strength and stiffness. The body of *Deinonychus* is so well structured for speed and high levels of activity that some scientists think it was a warm-blooded dinosaur, and that it may even have had feathers to aid it in retaining heat. Warm-bloodedness permits an animal to be very active. Birds (see p. 40) probably evolved from dinosaurs like *Deinonychus. Deinonychus* lived in the mid-Cretaceous, and is also known as *Velociraptor.* (61)

Deinonychus

42

ANKYLOSAURS

These four-footed dinosaurs of the middle and late Cretaceous were built along the same lines as an army tank! Their thick legs supported husky bodies well covered by thick bony scales, nodules, and spikes. These bulky dinosaurs survived by eating vegetation, clipping it with their beaklike mouths. If a carnosaur threatened an ankylosaur, it could defend itself by swinging its long, agile tail, tipped with a bony club. Like today's rhinos, ankylosaurs could move with surprising speed in spite of their bulk. All were ornithischians (bird-hipped dinosaurs).

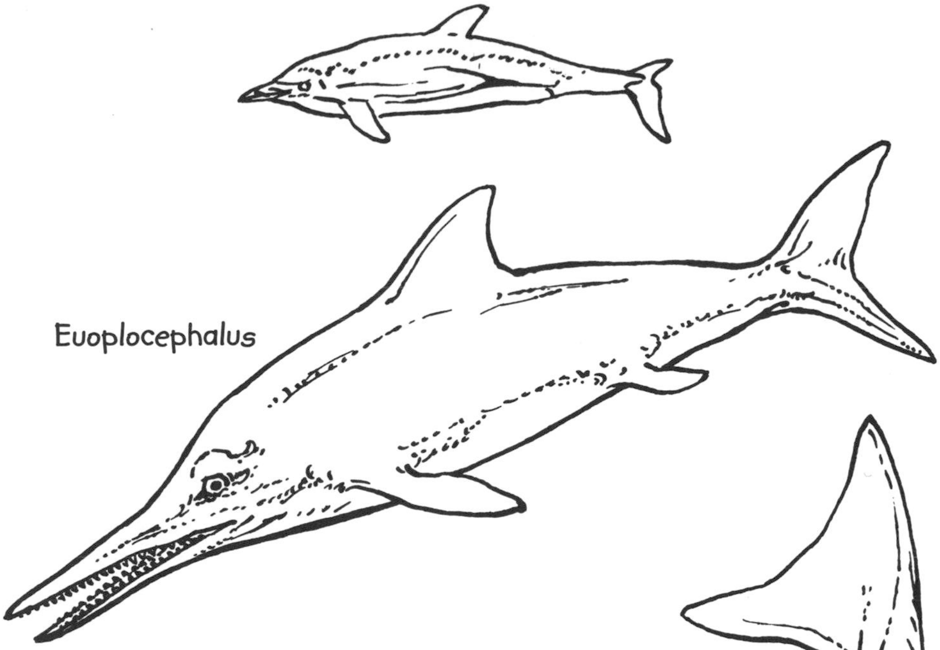

Euoplocephalus

Euoplocephalus To 20 feet. This large ankylosaur from western North America would easily dwarf a full-sized automobile. It weighed up to 3 tons. The skull was very bony, and the teeth were very small. **(62)**

Nodosaurus To 18 feet. Nodosaurs were less bulky and possibly less agile than their larger relatives, the ankylosaurs. They lacked the club-tipped tail but had armorlike skin over part of their backs. Some had large spikes along their sides. Nodosaurs are less well known than ankylosaurs. **(63)**

Nodosaurus

43

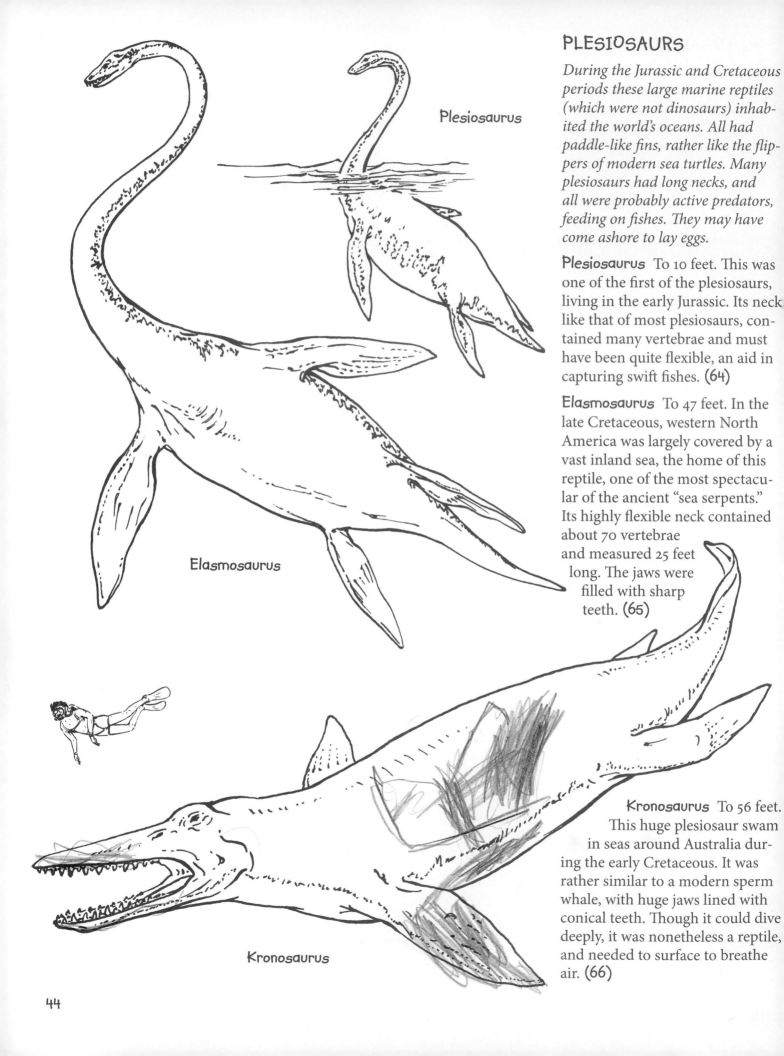

Plesiosaurus

Elasmosaurus

Kronosaurus

PLESIOSAURS

During the Jurassic and Cretaceous periods these large marine reptiles (which were not dinosaurs) inhabited the world's oceans. All had paddle-like fins, rather like the flippers of modern sea turtles. Many plesiosaurs had long necks, and all were probably active predators, feeding on fishes. They may have come ashore to lay eggs.

Plesiosaurus To 10 feet. This was one of the first of the plesiosaurs, living in the early Jurassic. Its neck like that of most plesiosaurs, contained many vertebrae and must have been quite flexible, an aid in capturing swift fishes. (64)

Elasmosaurus To 47 feet. In the late Cretaceous, western North America was largely covered by a vast inland sea, the home of this reptile, one of the most spectacular of the ancient "sea serpents." Its highly flexible neck contained about 70 vertebrae and measured 25 feet long. The jaws were filled with sharp teeth. (65)

Kronosaurus To 56 feet. This huge plesiosaur swam in seas around Australia during the early Cretaceous. It was rather similar to a modern sperm whale, with huge jaws lined with conical teeth. Though it could dive deeply, it was nonetheless a reptile, and needed to surface to breathe air. (66)

ICHTHYOSAURS

The name ichthyosaur means "fish-lizard," a good description of these aquatic reptiles of the Mesozoic era. They closely resembled fishes in body form, though they breathed air, as do all reptiles. Modern whales and porpoises, all of which are mammals, also have a fishlike body form and breathe air. Ichthyosaurs, marine mammals, and fishes independently evolved a streamlined body form with fins or flippers, in response to the same aquatic environment. Fossils indicate that ichthyosaurs gave birth to live young.

Ichthyosaurus To 10 feet. This swift, streamlined animal could swim efficiently in pursuit of fishes. Its jaws were elongated and lined with sharp teeth. Notice how similar ichthyosaurs were to porpoises, though their reptilian brains were not nearly as large as those of the aquatic mammals. **(67)**

Shonisaurus To 50 feet. At 40 tons, with a 10-foot-long skull and eyeballs fully 12 inches in diameter, this was by far the largest of the ichthyosaurs. It was similar to *Kronosaurus* (see p. 44) in general anatomy but lived long before it, in the Triassic period. *Shonisaurus* may well have been the largest creature of the Triassic. **(68)**

PLACODONTS

These early aquatic reptiles resembled modern marine iguanas like the ones found on the Galápagos Islands.

Placodus To 6 feet. This husky placodont fed on clams and mussels, using its blunt, peglike teeth. **(69)**

Porpoise

Ichthyosaurus

Shonisaurus

Placodus

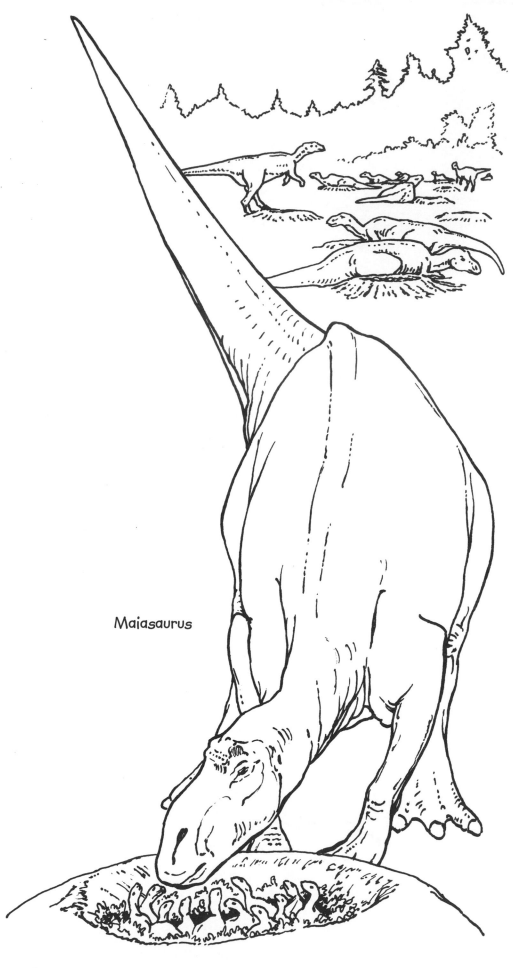

Maiasaurus

DINOSAUR NESTING BEHAVIOR

How dinosaurs reproduced and reared their young was once a great mystery. Now the answers are at least partially known. Fossil eggs have been found from several dinosaurs, including the ones we show on this page and the next. Like birds and crocodiles, to which they were closely related, most dinosaurs laid eggs. They also scraped out nests, and parents tended their hatchlings. Some dinosaurs nested in colonies, like modern gulls and terns.

Maiasaurus To 30 feet. The name of this Cretaceous dinosaur means "mother lizard." This was an apt choice, since its fossils include eggs, hatchlings, and juveniles as well as adults. A nesting colony of maiasaurs lived along a river nearly 80 million years ago in what is now Montana. The adults stood nearly 15 feet tall, and babies were 1 foot tall and 3 feet long at hatching. Each clutch of 20 eggs was contained in a mud nest 6 feet in diameter. Herds of adult and juvenile maiasaurs fed on vegetation, and the adults probably protected the young from marauding carnosaurs. Maiasaurs were duck-billed dinosaurs (see pp. 50–51). **(70)**

Protoceratops To 6 feet. This small, four-legged dinosaur lived in Outer Mongolia. In 1922, scientists from the American Museum of Natural History discovered fossilized nests, eggs, and young of *Protoceratops* during a historic expedition to the Gobi Desert. In a remote area of the desert known as Flaming Cliffs, they found dozens of skeletons and eggs embedded in the striking red sandstone. The skeletons were of animals of all ages, and some of the eggs were still arranged in circular patterns in the fossilized nests. These were the first dinosaur eggs ever discovered. Like the maiasaurs in Montana, these small dinosaurs may have gathered in colonies to reproduce.

Protoceratops lived in the mid-Cretaceous and was one of the first of the ceratopsid

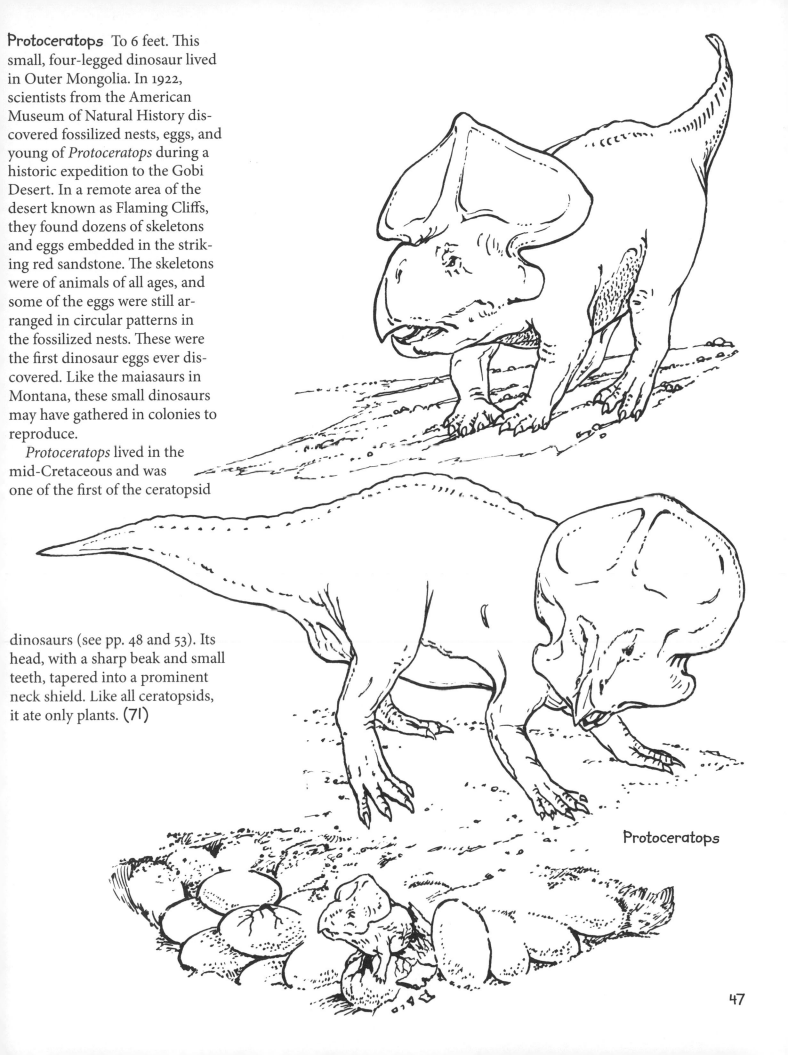

dinosaurs (see pp. 48 and 53). Its head, with a sharp beak and small teeth, tapered into a prominent neck shield. Like all ceratopsids, it ate only plants. (71)

Protoceratops

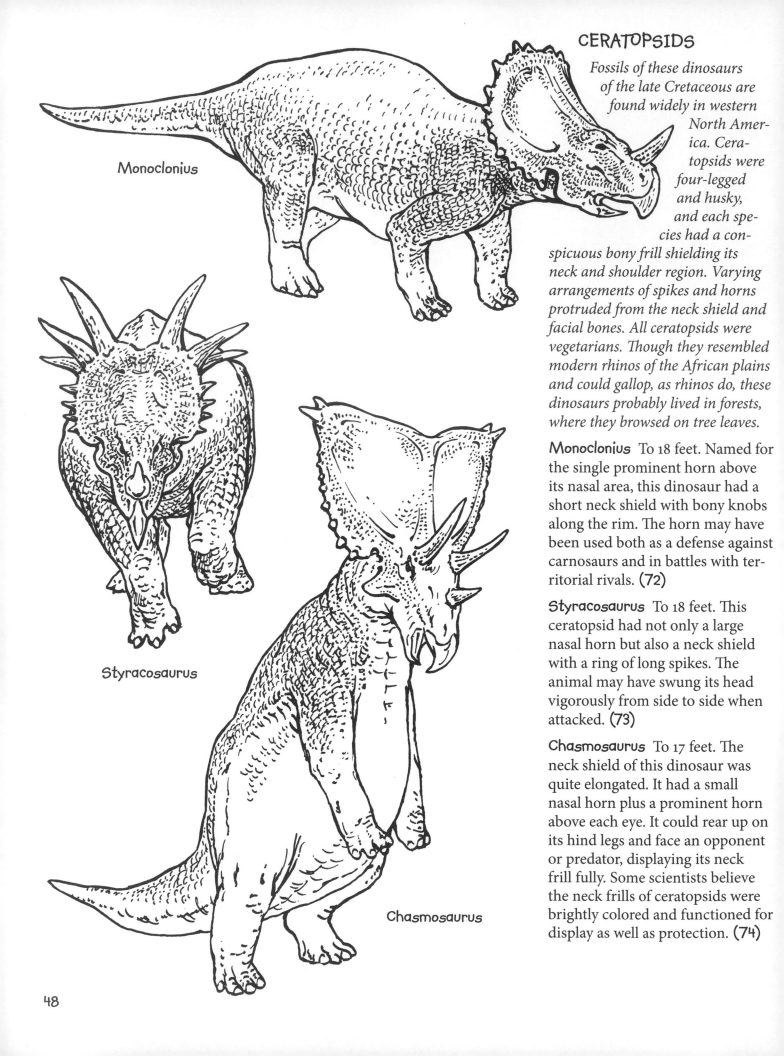

CERATOPSIDS

Fossils of these dinosaurs of the late Cretaceous are found widely in western North America. Ceratopsids were four-legged and husky, and each species had a conspicuous bony frill shielding its neck and shoulder region. Varying arrangements of spikes and horns protruded from the neck shield and facial bones. All ceratopsids were vegetarians. Though they resembled modern rhinos of the African plains and could gallop, as rhinos do, these dinosaurs probably lived in forests, where they browsed on tree leaves.

Monoclonius To 18 feet. Named for the single prominent horn above its nasal area, this dinosaur had a short neck shield with bony knobs along the rim. The horn may have been used both as a defense against carnosaurs and in battles with territorial rivals. **(72)**

Styracosaurus To 18 feet. This ceratopsid had not only a large nasal horn but also a neck shield with a ring of long spikes. The animal may have swung its head vigorously from side to side when attacked. **(73)**

Chasmosaurus To 17 feet. The neck shield of this dinosaur was quite elongated. It had a small nasal horn plus a prominent horn above each eye. It could rear up on its hind legs and face an opponent or predator, displaying its neck frill fully. Some scientists believe the neck frills of ceratopsids were brightly colored and functioned for display as well as protection. **(74)**

Monoclonius

Styracosaurus

Chasmosaurus

ORNITHOPODS

Ornithopods were a diverse and abundant group of ornithischians (bird-hipped dinosaurs). They lived on land and were found on most of the continents during the Jurassic and Cretaceous periods. There were many kinds of ornithopods, but the most prominent were the iguanodontids and hadrosaurids. Both groups lived during the Cretaceous. Ornithopods had large hind legs and could easily rear up. Many were probably bipedal (two-legged), but they may have used their strong arms to walk on all fours. These dinosaurs ate only plant material.

Iguanodon To 30 feet. *Iguanodon* was the first dinosaur to be described when Dr. Gideon Mantell

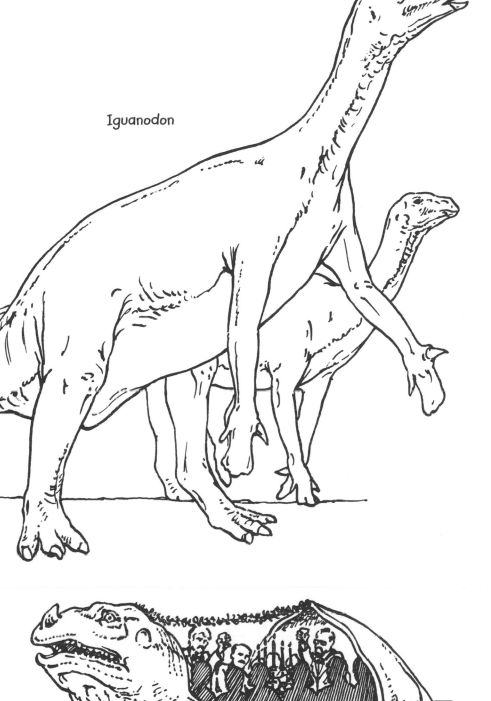

Iguanodon

brought it to the world's attention in 1822. Actually, his wife found the fossils, some odd teeth, near Brighton, England. Baron Cuvier, France's leading anatomist, thought the teeth resembled those of a giant iguana, hence the name *Iguanodon* (iguana-tooth). Later, when skeletons were unearthed, both Cuvier and Richard Owen, England's premier anatomist, placed the thumb spike on the nose, like a rhino's horn. *Iguanodon* was restored as though it were a giant lizard shaped like a rhino. *Iguanodon*'s great size was of major interest to the public, and a full-sized restoration was once used as a dining room by a group of 20 prominent British scientists! Many skeletons have been found, evidence that iguanodontids ranged widely over the earth. Males were larger than females, and both sexes fed together in herds. **(75)**

49

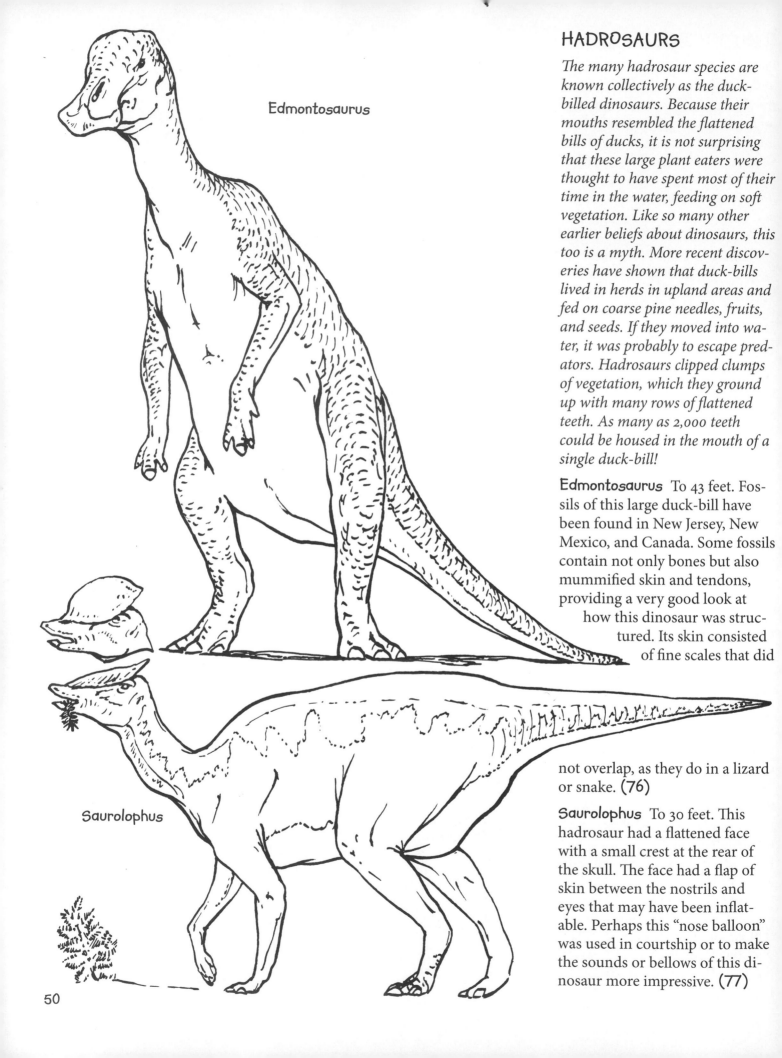

HADROSAURS

The many hadrosaur species are known collectively as the duck-billed dinosaurs. Because their mouths resembled the flattened bills of ducks, it is not surprising that these large plant eaters were thought to have spent most of their time in the water, feeding on soft vegetation. Like so many other earlier beliefs about dinosaurs, this too is a myth. More recent discoveries have shown that duck-bills lived in herds in upland areas and fed on coarse pine needles, fruits, and seeds. If they moved into water, it was probably to escape predators. Hadrosaurs clipped clumps of vegetation, which they ground up with many rows of flattened teeth. As many as 2,000 teeth could be housed in the mouth of a single duck-bill!

Edmontosaurus To 43 feet. Fossils of this large duck-bill have been found in New Jersey, New Mexico, and Canada. Some fossils contain not only bones but also mummified skin and tendons, providing a very good look at how this dinosaur was structured. Its skin consisted of fine scales that did not overlap, as they do in a lizard or snake. (76)

Saurolophus To 30 feet. This hadrosaur had a flattened face with a small crest at the rear of the skull. The face had a flap of skin between the nostrils and eyes that may have been inflatable. Perhaps this "nose balloon" was used in courtship or to make the sounds or bellows of this dinosaur more impressive. (77)

Edmontosaurus

Saurolophus

50

CRESTED DUCK-BILLS

Many duck-bill species had elaborate crests of bone on their heads. These bones contained nasal passages and may have helped the animal make loud trumpeting sounds or detect odors. The odd shapes and unique sounds may have helped species to recognize each other. An old belief was that the crests were used to store air while the animal was underwater. This is no longer considered likely.

Each of the three crested hadrosaurs described here lived during the late Cretaceous in what is now Alberta, Canada. Perhaps they foraged in mixed herds, as African antelopes do today.

Parasaurolophus To 33 feet. This dinosaur had a crest over 3 feet long extending beyond its skull. Air traveled from nostrils, located at the tip of the snout, all the way up and down the crest before moving to the throat and lungs. (78)

Corythosaurus To 33 feet. The disklike crest on this large hadrosaur was most pronounced in males, and smaller in females and juveniles. (79)

Lambeosaurus To 40 feet. The crest of this hadrosaur was almost hatchetlike, with the "blade" over the nose and the "handle" extending beyond the skull. (80)

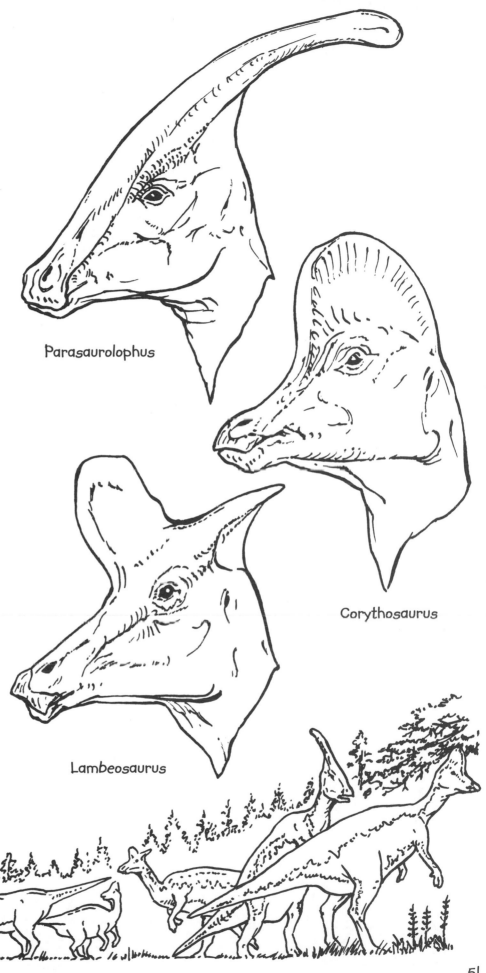

Parasaurolophus

Corythosaurus

Lambeosaurus

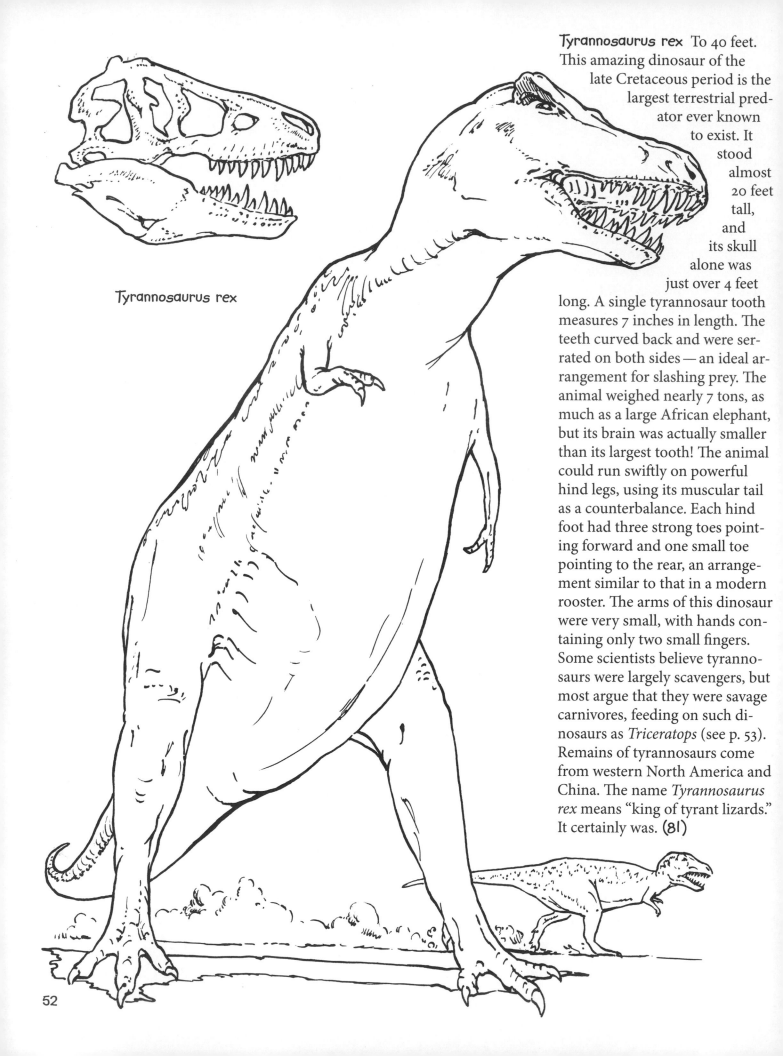

Tyrannosaurus rex

Tyrannosaurus rex To 40 feet. This amazing dinosaur of the late Cretaceous period is the largest terrestrial predator ever known to exist. It stood almost 20 feet tall, and its skull alone was just over 4 feet long. A single tyrannosaur tooth measures 7 inches in length. The teeth curved back and were serrated on both sides — an ideal arrangement for slashing prey. The animal weighed nearly 7 tons, as much as a large African elephant, but its brain was actually smaller than its largest tooth! The animal could run swiftly on powerful hind legs, using its muscular tail as a counterbalance. Each hind foot had three strong toes pointing forward and one small toe pointing to the rear, an arrangement similar to that in a modern rooster. The arms of this dinosaur were very small, with hands containing only two small fingers. Some scientists believe tyrannosaurs were largely scavengers, but most argue that they were savage carnivores, feeding on such dinosaurs as *Triceratops* (see p. 53). Remains of tyrannosaurs come from western North America and China. The name *Tyrannosaurus rex* means "king of tyrant lizards." It certainly was. **(81)**

Triceratops To 30 feet. During the late Cretaceous, many herds of the 6-ton *Triceratops,* or "three-horned face," galloped over what is now the American West. This was one of the last of the dinosaurs, quite possibly *the* last species to exist. The long horn above each eye measured up to 3 feet in length and may have been even longer. All that remains of them are bony cores, but in life each horn may have been covered by additional material, as they are in modern sheep and goats. A herd of *Triceratops* would have been no easy prey for a hungry *Tyrannosaurus.* Like African rhinos today, an adult *Triceratops* was able to run from danger or face it with a strong offense.

Fossil locations show that these dinosaurs probably inhabited forests of redwoods and other tall trees. They ate only plant food, which they cropped with their beaklike mouths and ground up with flattened, molarlike teeth. **(82)**

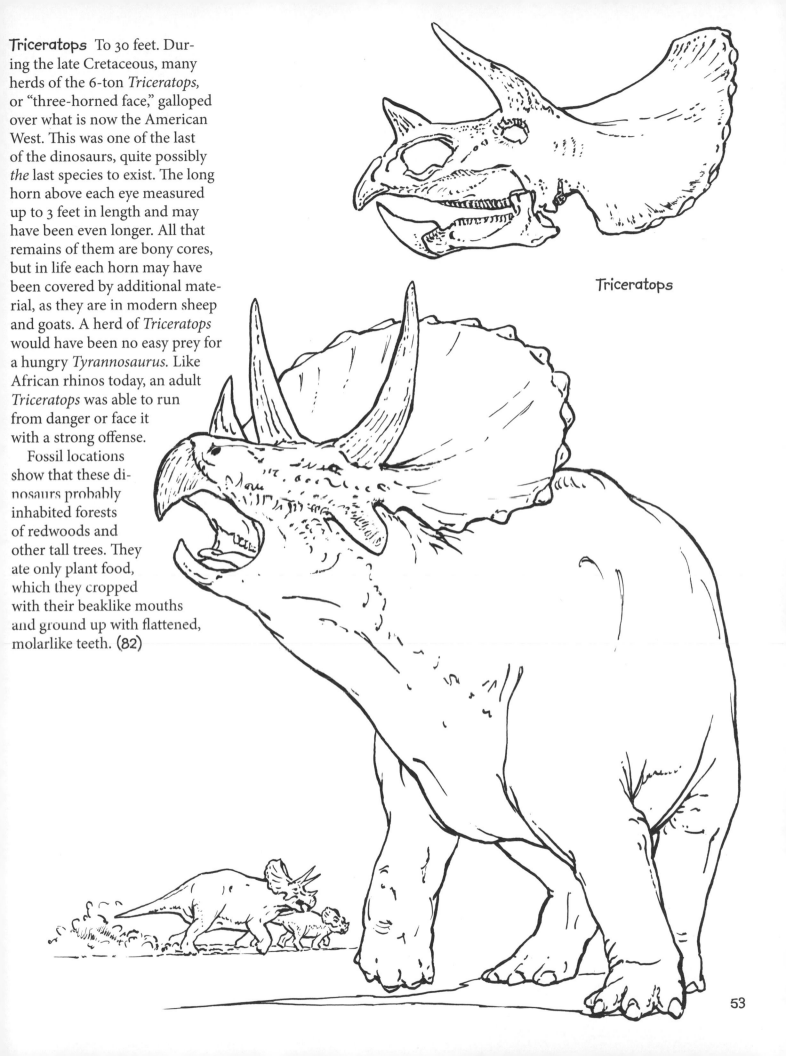

Triceratops

53

THE END OF THE DINOSAURS

Did dinosaurs go out with a bang or a whimper? Actually, they probably did both. All we know for certain is that the great reptilian creatures of the Mesozoic have left no traces after the close of the Cretaceous period, 65 million years ago. Though modern birds may be thought of by some as feathered dinosaurs (see introduction and p. 40), the immense tyrannosaurs, ceratopsids, duckbills, and sauropods are long gone. So are the ichthyosaurs, plesiosaurs, and mosasaurs, as well as the flying pterosaurs. The land, sea, and sky were far less populated after the Cretaceous. What happened? What killed the dinosaurs? The fossil record indicates that most dinosaurs had already become extinct before the end of the Cretaceous. Dinosaurs were becoming gradually less abundant and diverse long before their final disappearance. The climate was changing, becoming more temperate, and perhaps most species failed to adapt to the changes. Perhaps new diseases or parasites were afflicting dinosaur species.

However, the sudden and large-scale extinction that took place at the very end of the Cretaceous, and affected not only dinosaurs but many other kinds of animals, including many marine species, seems to indicate that some sweeping catastrophic event took place. Evidence from geology supports the hypothesis that such an event did, in fact, occur. It is possible that an asteroid (a small, planetlike body about 5 to 6 miles in diameter) or a comet collided with Earth 65 million years ago, causing severe and sudden climatic changes that led to the numerous extinctions. Scientists differ as to the effects of such a cosmic collision. Most say that the Earth got much darker and cooler, but some argue that the Earth suddenly warmed. In either case, conditions would no longer have been suitable for most animals, thus the Cretaceous extinctions. Large-scale volcanic activity may also have been occurring, and it could have triggered climatic changes similar to those ascribed to the supposed cosmic collision. Use your imagination to color this scene, as you contemplate the final days of the dinosaurs.

54

MAMMAL-LIKE REPTILES

Both dinosaurs and mammals evolved from ancient reptiles, but the reptile ancestors of the mammals were quite distinct from the reptiles that were ancestors of dinosaurs. Mammals descended from a diverse group of sprawling creatures that were known as mammal-like reptiles *because their skull bones, jaws, and teeth bear a close similarity to those of mammals. Modern mammals have a body covering of hair and suckle their young with milk, but since these features do not leave fossils, we are uncertain as to when they evolved. Mammal-like reptiles lived before dinosaurs, in the Permian period (see p. 10), and survived through much of the Triassic. They eventually became extinct but first gave rise to true mammals.*

Pelycosaurs To 11 feet. Some of the first mammal-like reptiles had long spines projecting from their backbones. When the animal was alive, these spines were enclosed by a membrane of skin, much like the fin on a modern-day sailfish. No one knows why such a structure was present but it may have been a solar panel, absorbing and radiating heat to help the animal warm up or cool down. We illustrate two well-known pelycosaurs: *Dimetrodon,* a large carnivore with formidable slashing teeth (83), and *Edaphosaurus,* a small-headed plant eater with peglike teeth. (84)

Dimetrodon

Edaphosaurus

56

THERAPSIDS

These mammal-like reptiles became increasingly similar to true mammals and finally gave rise to them.

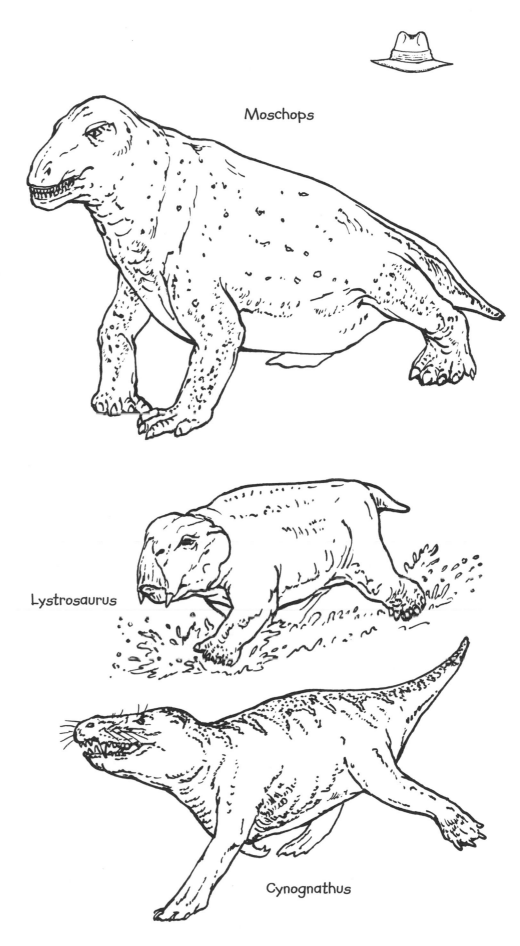

Moschops

Moschops To 8 feet. Imagine a toad about the size of a sedan and you get some idea of a *Moschops*. This lumbering plant eater belonged to a group called the dinocephalians. As hard as it may be to believe, these were the antelopes and rhinos of their day. Many *Moschops* and their relatives grazed in what is now South Africa in the mid-Permian period. **(85)**

Lystrosaurus To 3 feet. Fossils of this small, mammal-like reptile have been found in India, South Africa, China, and Antarctica. Such a wide distribution for a small land-dwelling animal helped supply evidence that Earth's continents were joined together in one large mass back in the Permian. Since then they have drifted on huge plates, coming to occupy their present positions. *Lystrosaurus* was a dicynodont, meaning "double dog-tooth," a reference to its two upper canine teeth. Despite the canines, this creature ate only plants. **(86)**

Lystrosaurus

Cynognathus To 5 feet. Though considered to be a reptile, *Cynognathus* (whose name means "dog-jawed") would have looked very much like a primitive wolf. It belonged to a group called the theriodonts, meaning "beast-toothed." Its skull and teeth were almost mammalian, and it may have been warm-blooded and covered with fur. Its limbs and overall body shape were similar to those of true mammals, which are, indeed, evolved from advanced theriodonts. *Cynognathus* lived in the mid-Triassic and was a carnivore, the wolf of its day. **(87)**

Cynognathus

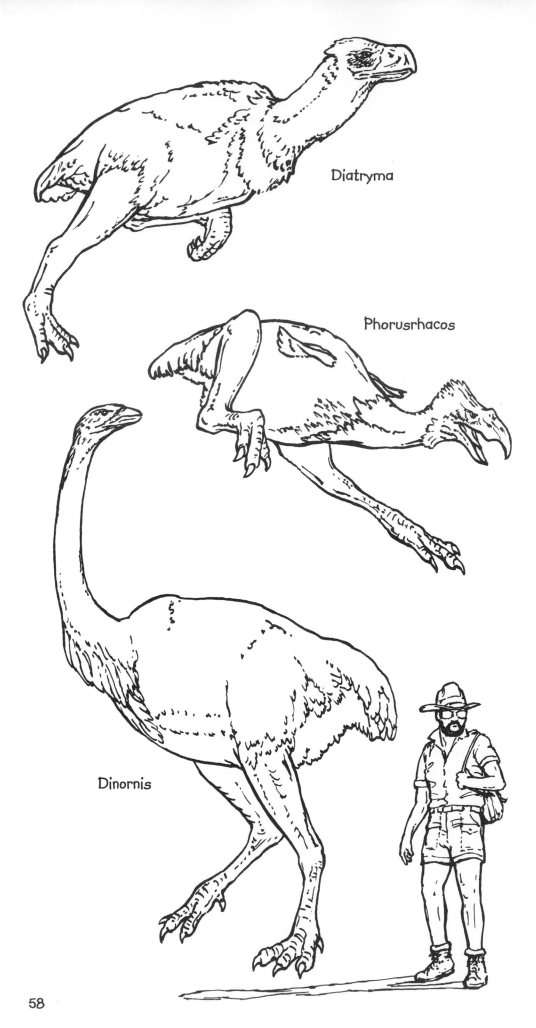

Diatryma

Phorusrhacos

Dinornis

BIG BAD BIRDS

The end of the Cretaceous period and the extinction of the great dinosaurs left a void. Soon the evolving mammals replaced the giant reptiles. However, for a brief time at the beginning of the Cenozoic era (see p. 11), birds were among the most important carnivores. These big birds chased, captured, and fed on the little mammals that were the Mesozoic survivors.

Diatryma To 6 feet tall. This huge predatory bird roamed the North American plains 50 million years ago. With an immense hawklike bill and powerful running legs, it must have been one of the largest carnivores of its time. (88)

Phorusrhacos To 6 feet tall. As *Diatryma* roamed among the diminutive mammals of North America, so did *Phorusrhacos* in South America. This giant bird lived about 20 million years ago in what is now Argentina and Chile. (89)

Though both *Diatryma* and *Phorusrhacos* were top predators of their time, each was a far cry from their carnivorous predecessors, like *Tyrannosaurus*.

Dinornis To 11½ feet tall. Though big, this bird threatened no one. It belonged to a group called the moas, all of which lived in New Zealand. These birds, which fed entirely on plants, became extinct only about 400 years ago. The Maori peoples of New Zealand overhunted them. Their only survivor is the flightless kiwi, a close relative. (90)

EARLY CENOZOIC MAMMALS

Mammals have a rich fossil history. The horses, elephants, camels, and lions of today all have ancestors in the fossil record. Here are a few examples of small furred creatures that lived very long ago and to which some modern species trace their genetic roots.

Hyracotherium To 2 feet. A horse the size of a terrier? Indeed, as odd as it may seem, the first horse was a dainty five-toed animal that bore faint resemblance to the one-toed thoroughbreds of today. Horses of many species lived during the Cenozoic, but little *Hyracotherium* (also called *Eohippus*, the "dawn horse") was the first. It lived in North America, where it fed on leaves. **(91)**

Moeritherium To 5 feet. This husky, sheep-sized creature was the ancestor of the proboscideans, or elephants. Its short snout gave little indication of the long, flexible trunk that would characterize its massive descendants. Fossils come from northern Africa. **(92)**

Phenacodus To 4 feet. About the size of a goat, to which it is very distantly related, this animal was the first true hoofed mammal. It was a condylarth, the group of plant eaters from which all hoofed or ungulate mammals evolved. Its fossils come from Europe and North America. **(93)**

Patriofelis To 6 feet. Just as the plant-eating mammals diversified, so did the meat eaters. *Patriofelis* was an early creodont, one of the mammals that gave rise to bears, cats, dogs, and other carnivores. It hunted its prey in North America nearly 60 million years ago. **(94)**

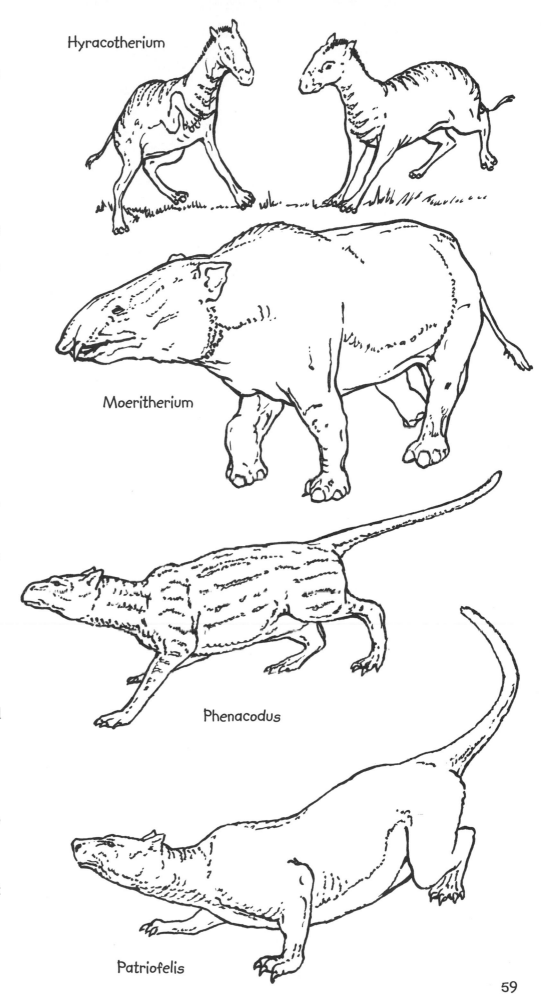

Hyracotherium

Moeritherium

Phenacodus

Patriofelis

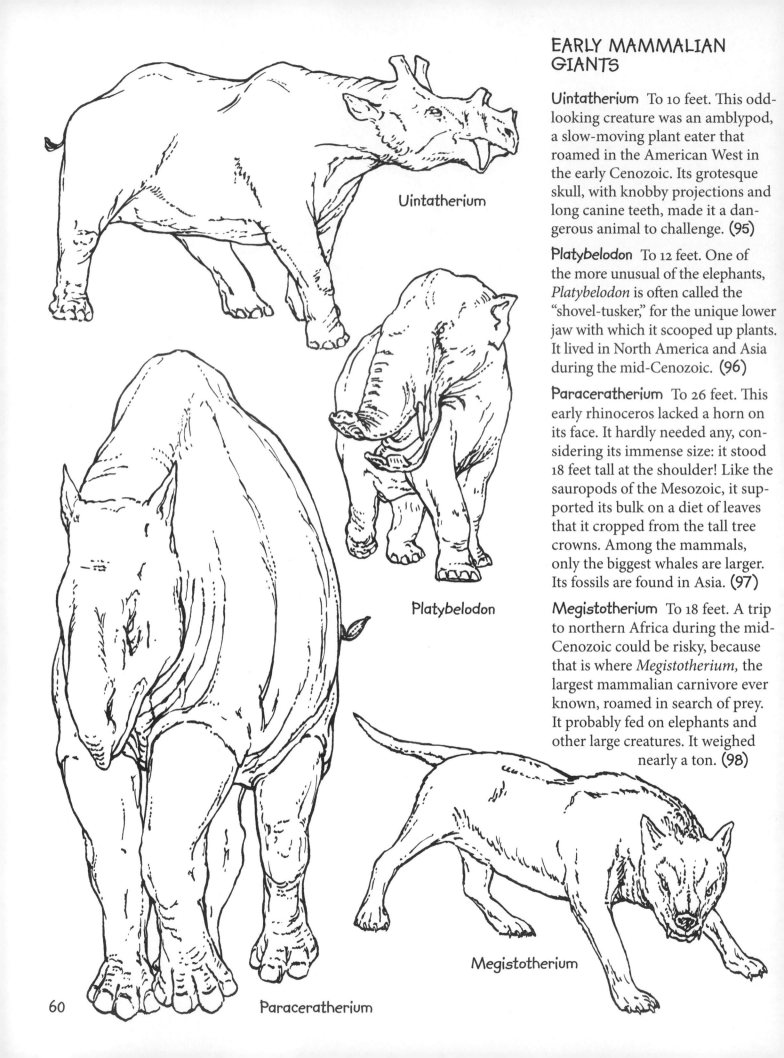

EARLY MAMMALIAN GIANTS

Uintatherium To 10 feet. This odd-looking creature was an amblypod, a slow-moving plant eater that roamed in the American West in the early Cenozoic. Its grotesque skull, with knobby projections and long canine teeth, made it a dangerous animal to challenge. **(95)**

Platybelodon To 12 feet. One of the more unusual of the elephants, *Platybelodon* is often called the "shovel-tusker," for the unique lower jaw with which it scooped up plants. It lived in North America and Asia during the mid-Cenozoic. **(96)**

Paraceratherium To 26 feet. This early rhinoceros lacked a horn on its face. It hardly needed any, considering its immense size: it stood 18 feet tall at the shoulder! Like the sauropods of the Mesozoic, it supported its bulk on a diet of leaves that it cropped from the tall tree crowns. Among the mammals, only the biggest whales are larger. Its fossils are found in Asia. **(97)**

Megistotherium To 18 feet. A trip to northern Africa during the mid-Cenozoic could be risky, because that is where *Megistotherium,* the largest mammalian carnivore ever known, roamed in search of prey. It probably fed on elephants and other large creatures. It weighed nearly a ton. **(98)**

Uintatherium

Platybelodon

Megistotherium

Paraceratherium

SOUTH AMERICAN GIANTS

Several impressively large mammals lived in South America just prior to and during the Ice Age.

Toxodon To 10 feet. A *Toxodon* was a lumbering, plant-eating beast that resembled a combination of rhino and pig. Its bulk was probably its major protection. It snipped off leaves with sharp incisor teeth and ground them up with large molars. It belonged to a group called the notoungulates, found only in South America. **(99)**

Glyptodon To 10 feet. Related to the armadillos, which it vaguely resembled, the *Glyptodon* was a sort of huge mammalian tortoise. Protected by its dense bony covering, it plodded along munching plants. If irritated, it could swing its clublike tail. Compare it with the ankylosaurs (see p. 43). **(100)**

Megatherium To 20 feet. Appropriately called the giant ground sloth, *Megatherium* could rear up on its hind legs to reach treetop vegetation. Though quite large, it bore a close similarity to today's much smaller tree sloths, a fact that influenced Charles Darwin in his thinking about evolution. **(101)**

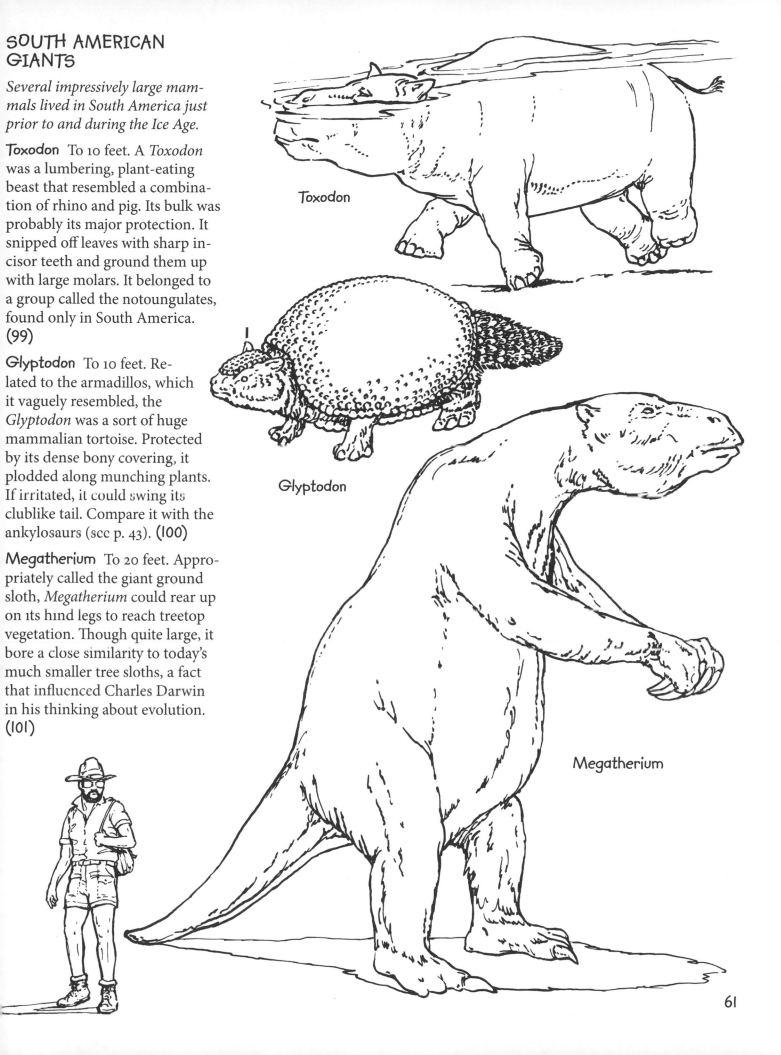

Toxodon

Glyptodon

Megatherium

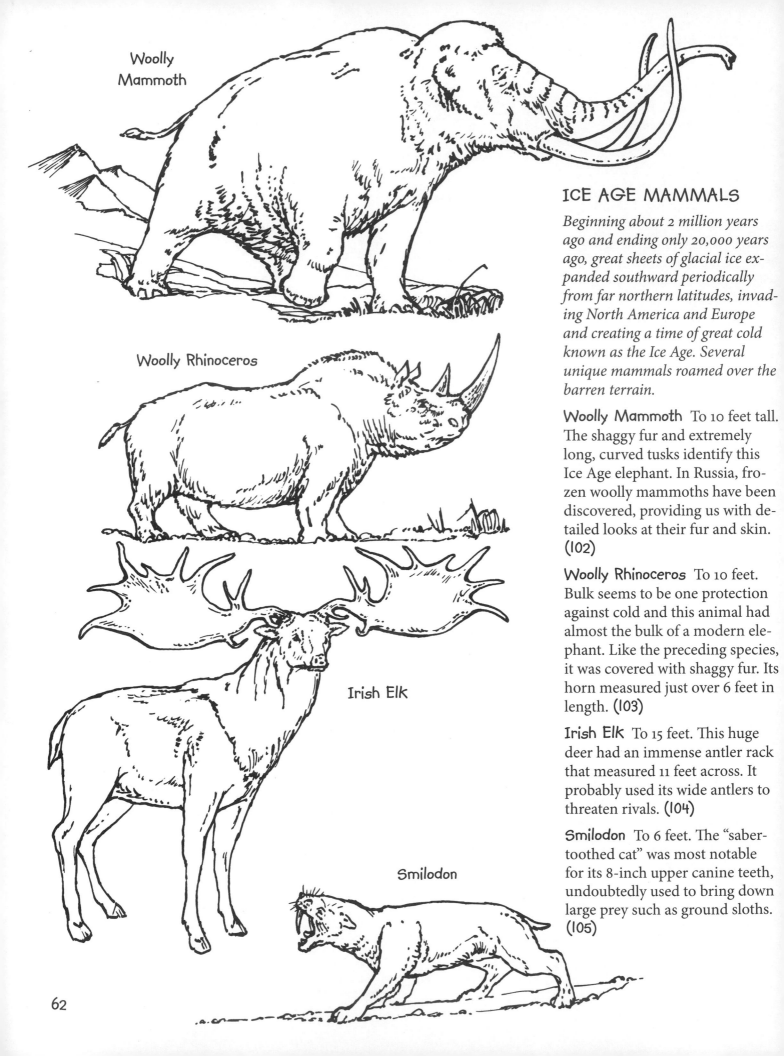

Woolly
Mammoth

Woolly Rhinoceros

Irish Elk

Smilodon

ICE AGE MAMMALS

Beginning about 2 million years ago and ending only 20,000 years ago, great sheets of glacial ice expanded southward periodically from far northern latitudes, invading North America and Europe and creating a time of great cold known as the Ice Age. Several unique mammals roamed over the barren terrain.

Woolly Mammoth To 10 feet tall. The shaggy fur and extremely long, curved tusks identify this Ice Age elephant. In Russia, frozen woolly mammoths have been discovered, providing us with detailed looks at their fur and skin. (102)

Woolly Rhinoceros To 10 feet. Bulk seems to be one protection against cold and this animal had almost the bulk of a modern elephant. Like the preceding species, it was covered with shaggy fur. Its horn measured just over 6 feet in length. (103)

Irish Elk To 15 feet. This huge deer had an immense antler rack that measured 11 feet across. It probably used its wide antlers to threaten rivals. (104)

Smilodon To 6 feet. The "saber-toothed cat" was most notable for its 8-inch upper canine teeth, undoubtedly used to bring down large prey such as ground sloths. (105)

HUMAN ANCESTORS

Given Earth's long history, humans are a recent species. Our ancestors originated in Africa, probably around 6 million years ago. Fossil remains tell us that there were several species of hominids that preceded our own species Homo sapiens.

Australopithecus afarensis

This small hominid is best known as the famous fossil "Lucy," a skeleton that is 40 percent complete and shows that *afarensis* walked fully upright, as we do. Fossil footprints have also been found, and they are no different from our own. Lucy's face would have somewhat resembled that of a chimpanzee, with a brain only about one-third as large as ours. Lucy and her family lived about 3.5 million years ago in East Africa. **(106)**

Paranthropus boisei

Larger and more robust than little afarensis, *Paranthropus* inhabited east Africa until about 1.5 million years ago. The large jaws and teeth indicate that *Paranthropus* ate coarse plant material. **(107)**

Homo erectus

Homo erectus evolved in Africa but spread over Europe and Asia, persisting until about 500,000 years ago. These hominids lived in cooperative groups that made and used tools, and probably used fire to cook. Their brain size was nearly three-fourths that of modern humans. Our species is probably directly descended from *Homo erectus*. **(108)**

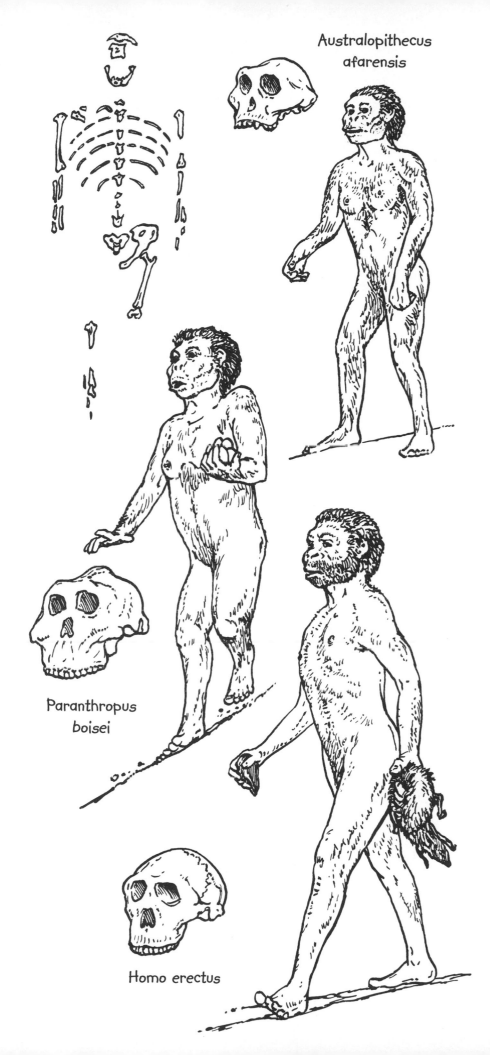

Australopithecus afarensis

Paranthropus boisei

Homo erectus

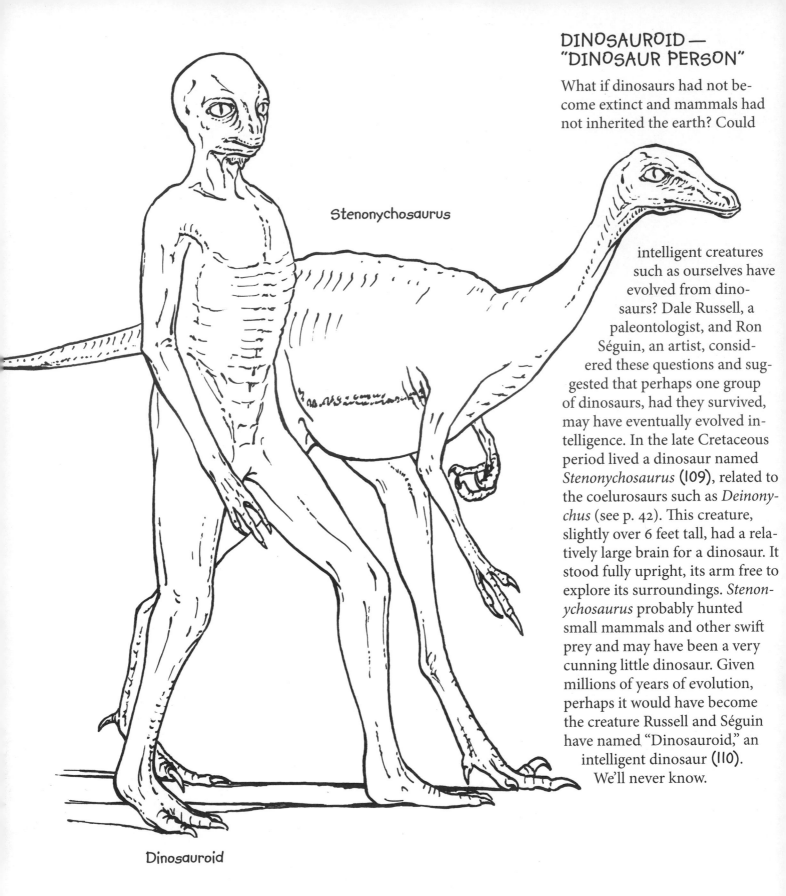

DINOSAUROID—"DINOSAUR PERSON"

What if dinosaurs had not become extinct and mammals had not inherited the earth? Could intelligent creatures such as ourselves have evolved from dinosaurs? Dale Russell, a paleontologist, and Ron Séguin, an artist, considered these questions and suggested that perhaps one group of dinosaurs, had they survived, may have eventually evolved intelligence. In the late Cretaceous period lived a dinosaur named *Stenonychosaurus* (109), related to the coelurosaurs such as *Deinonychus* (see p. 42). This creature, slightly over 6 feet tall, had a relatively large brain for a dinosaur. It stood fully upright, its arm free to explore its surroundings. *Stenonychosaurus* probably hunted small mammals and other swift prey and may have been a very cunning little dinosaur. Given millions of years of evolution, perhaps it would have become the creature Russell and Séguin have named "Dinosauroid," an intelligent dinosaur (110). We'll never know.

Stenonychosaurus

Dinosauroid